HUMANS WITHOUT BORDERS

MADHAVA KUMAR TURUMELLA

BLUEROSE PUBLISHERS

India | U.K.

For permissions requests or inquiries regarding this publication,
please contact:

BLUEROSE PUBLISHERS
www.BlueRoseONE.com
info@bluerosepublishers.com
+91 8882 898 898
+4407342408967

ISBN: 978-93-5819-145-5

Cover design: Tahira Akhtar
Typesetting: Namrata Saini

First Edition: July 2023

DEDICATION

To all the Hapless Refugees, rich and poor, of this world.

EPIGRAPH

'It is not for nothing that our age cries out for the redeemer personality, for the one who can emancipate himself from the grip of the collective and save at least his own soul, who lights a beacon of hope for others, proclaiming that here is at least one man who has succeeded in extricating himself from the fatal identity with the group psyche.'

Carl Jung, Civilisation in Transition (Jung, n.d., p.154) [1]

TABLE OF CONTENTS

PREAMBLE

Humans without Borders is a series of thoughts I have been contemplating for decades. But the burning desire within me to publish my thoughts in a book started at the end of 2015. In that year, The United Nations invited me to Turkey and other countries in the Middle East to participate as a speaker in seminars jointly organised by the UN and respective countries. In Turkey, the conference was about interfaith and global climate change. Like the rest of the world, I am also apprehensive about the climate crisis. The United Nations is my favourite international organisation, which I believe is capable of helping shape the world and making it a safe place to live for future generations.

While in Turkey, I witnessed scores of children refugees near the airport. It was the time the world was facing the ISIS calamity. A child told me that they had walked from Iraq, hundreds of miles of walking. My heart wept, thinking what an ordeal it must be in such a small child's life. No child is in control of the events that happen to them. But the adult world bears the direct responsibility for every child in trouble. Also, during my discussions with other delegates at the UN interfaith climate conference, I learned first-hand of the calamities faced by refugees from Africa and around the world.

The priest in me was very much troubled. Priests from all religions earnestly pray for world peace, but how is it that the world still suffers so many calamities? Where are we falling?

As a child and when growing up, I also faced a series of unfortunate events. The abuse I faced traumatised me. Therefore, I can relate to the traumatic events many children undergo. Any trauma leaves a profound impact on the soul.

When children face trauma, it breaks the trust cycle in them. They grow up not trusting the terrifying adult world. But all children eventually grow up. Traumatised children grow up biologically, but by that time, their trauma has confused them, and they have become. untrusting and scared at the level of the soul.

Children who grow up in traumatic backgrounds do misbehave. While growing up and as adults, some are fortunate enough to get help from psychotherapy and other forms of healing to heal themselves. Some retreat into their shells, never willing to face the terrifying and brutal world. Some self-anaesthetise themselves with external substances to soothe their primal psychological wounds but tragically end up as drug addicts. Some prematurely end their life. Some become split personalities, and others remain as 'adult children'.

It is clear that the childhood over which these unfortunate children had no control will impact their adult life. Therefore it is essential to protect not only refugee children but all children worldwide. We must aspire to provide a trust circle for them. UNICEF is the proper organisation to make this happen.

Also, many extraordinary philanthropic individuals are trying to bring respite. Some donate money, and some others work as volunteers for various charities. The United Nations does monumental work in offering to help alleviate suffering in the world. Governments around the world do their bit to help. So I see a great intention to address the world's suffering. But the question is, Why are we still seeing so much crisis?! Who or what is causing this monumental human misery?! What forces are driving the climate crisis? What forces are compelling us to go to war? The world is sleepwalking from crisis to crisis. It appears that some miscreants keep causing arson around the world, and the good folks react by dousing the fires. But that is exhausting work. For sure, there must be some other way! Undoubtedly, it is we humans who have got it wrong.

Therefore, human behaviour intrigued me. What makes us human? What qualities are unique to us? Are we loving, caring, and sharing creatures by design, or are we lustful, hateful, and jealous animals? How can we enslave our own kind? Or misbehave towards our kind.

How can a human so blatantly try to exploit their fellow human?

The exploitative individual must think that the person they are victimising is stupid. Or the exploitative individuals must be undergoing cognitive dissonance, which I explain in detail in the later part of this book.

I tried to get an answer to the most important question I had, 'Why are we humans sabotaging our path towards our natural evolution?!'

I tried to get answers to intriguing human behaviour from traditional scriptures, from the Hindu scriptures in which I am formally trained and from the scriptures of other religions. For example, most Hindu scriptures are war stories; both Ramayana and Mahabharata narrate great battles. Also, if you visit any Hindu temple, you will notice that all Hindu gods and goddesses bear weapons. Yet most Hindus are known more for their non-violent easy-going public behaviour. And this intrigued me. Jesus Christ asked his followers to forgive their enemies. But we have seen in history how bloody and violent the Christian church was before the seventeenth century. People often erroneously claim Islam has spread through violence. I have a different view on how Islam has spread. I discussed these religions in the chapter 'The weaponisation of human needs'. There is a vast disconnect between what is preached in holy books and what is practised.

Not all humans follow a religion. Most people who say they have a religion do not take their faiths seriously. So human behaviour is much more complex than what religion explains it to be.

I used to be active in interfaith. I am a trained priest, and I studied many scriptures. But I still had many questions. To seek answers about intriguing human behaviour, I enrolled to train as a psychotherapist at the Institute of Psychosynthesis,. a school of transpersonal psychology founded by the Italian psychiatrist Dr Roberto Asagioli. I studied psychotherapy for four years before abandoning that endeavour in the final year. Because I felt so broken within myself, I felt unfit to guide another human out of their psychological misery! But I found the theoretical knowledge I gained as a trainee psychotherapist to be highly instrumental. It helped me to ground myself, and it gave me a perspective on what makes us human. My training in psychotherapy also shapes my thoughts and arguments in this book.

I did my graduation in finance, and then postgraduate studies in computer sciences. I am very much interested in business statistics. In the professional world, I am a data systems architect and I live in the professional world as a Data Systems Architect in Banking, Financial

Services, Insurance (BFSI), Pharmaceutical and Market Research domains. My passion for data analysis, advanced analytics, and systems architecture has also shaped some of the thoughts in this book.

I confess this is not an academic paper, nor am I adequately qualified to present an excellent analysis of the worldwide political and economic systems. But the seeker in me cannot sit quietly. I am an ordinary human, but I am inquisitive. I greatly desire to observe the world, read, and use that data to make sense of the world. Therefore, please treat this book as written by a friend, a well-wisher who wishes you and the world love, peace and prosperity.

In this book, I try to analyse the factors causing an ongoing crisis in humanity using a human-centric approach. Instead of using pure statistics and analysing the economics and wars causing concerns, I tried to analyse society using psychological and spiritual tools which I picked up during my training and formative years.

The urgency to write the book dawned upon me at the end of 2021. The year 2022 had been a painful experience for me, literally. Nearly every other day, a surgical needle penetrated my body. The medical staff drew my blood so many times I stopped counting. I was hospitalised multiple times for a couple of weeks and underwent two major surgical procedures. My physical body now bears huge permanent scars. What was being done was for my good. But the experience helped me look deep into myself. I became friends with my past-life karma. It held my hand in kind awareness and made me pull through.

I was desperately looking to divert my mind from the agony I was experiencing. So I thought, 'Why not write the book I want to write?'. And I started writing this book. It helped me divert my mind. As I told you, the book is about my thoughts towards humanity. I wish all humanity to come together in love, feel peace and share prosperity. I seek a new social architecture to build the world. I want to think about a kind of Humanity version 2.0, upgraded to remove violence at all levels and instil peace. This book is my take on how we could make the world a better place to live, but there could be thoughts better than this. Therefore I welcome debate.

Another motivation behind writing this book is a story I heard in my childhood. Once upon a time, at the very beginning of time, this earth had only two inhabitants: a father and a mother. The couple had ten children. They loved all their children equally. As they grew old, they decided to distribute their wealth. They had ten acres of arable land as wealth. So they distributed the wealth equally. Each child inherited one acre of arable land. But, unfortunately, greed entered one of the children, and that child wanted to have one more acre for himself. But how could that be so?! The parents had given away all they had; distributing their land equally between their children. Therefore, the greedy child could not expect anything from them. But the child decided to steal from one of the vulnerable children who was physically weak, and deceived the weakest of the children, stealing the acre owned by the child. Thus, although parents distributed the wealth equally, the greed of one child made it doubly rich and one child landless.

Today's world economies serve the greedy, not the needy. Our interest rate systems work in support of those who are strongest amongst the human pack, as if helping to steal away from the weakest child!

The world systems, it appears, are only encouraging the rise of inequality. The purchasing power concentrated in the hands of exploitative individuals is causing a devastating impact on the whole of humanity.

The so-called leaders are statistically not true representatives of all people. The bureaucrats need to implement all people's wishes, but bureaucrats implement the desires of the so-called leaders. And because the leaders are not true leaders, the bureaucrats do not implement the wishes of all people. Therefore, having any countries or their respective borders is pointless.

All countries run reactive governance: we react after the event takes place, we investigate after the event, and we only make laws after something has gone out of control.

In this book, I propose removing all borders and demilitarising the whole world. Because if there are no countries or borders, we do not need any firepower. The military inventions of guns and mega firepower in the past century and the brain-hacking technologies of this century have brought nothing but misery to humankind. Except for a few thousand individuals who use these destructive technologies, not even the countries they claim to represent, or the eight billion people who roam the earth, benefit from their wrongdoings.

We humans know how to fight. We know how to be destructive. We know how to manipulate, cheat, subvert. We know how to be pure evil. And we have fought against each other since the Stone Age and even before that! We are only improving our destructive techniques. But with all our scientific knowledge about this universe, why do we still fight?! For what? To what end?!

Our knowledge regarding super galaxies and our insignificant presence in this universe should have made us humble. But we fight each other because the 98% of us who wish for a peaceful living are divided into tribes, cultures, religions, languages, and food habits, culminating in countries and borders. And then, we allow exploitative and stupid individuals to dictate what is good and not suitable for us. The majority of humans are not involved in fighting! 98% of humanity does not bother fighting, even today. But that two per cent of persons yielding destructive power is engaged in fighting, and we are all hapless conscripts in their mad game of destruction and world wars.

Every human is born free. But we are not allowed to hold our own opinion or enjoy our freedom. Suppose one peace-loving individual's opinion is contrary to that of another violent power-loving individual. In that case, the peace-loving individual gets violently killed, or maimed, or his voice is suppressed. We get removed just like chess pawns are removed from the chessboard. Isn't that what happened to Socrates? Or to Jesus Christ? Or to President John F Kennedy? Or to Martin Luther King? Or to the many prophets and professors of peace around the world?

We fear violence so much that we automatically submit to those who harbour exploitative and violent tendencies. We give power to violently exploitative people and wonder why this world is not at peace. Thus, we live a life full of violence, restricting our progress towards peace. We need a global collective of non-violent thinking and altruistic doing. We must stop fighting and give love a chance to heal us. Therefore, this book is a proposal for lasting peace.

THE FOUR QUADRANTS OF HUMAN ACTIVITY

I would like you to do a small exercise. This exercise is aimed at understanding our modes of activity We all engage in various activities in our day-to-day life.

A human can think whatever they want, but when that thought becomes an action, that action often falls into one of the four quadrants that will affect fellow humans.

Think of one of the major activities you will undertake today or in the immediate future. For example, signing a business deal, participating in a protest, giving away money to a charity, taking a decision about someone, starting a new business venture, etc.

Every significant action involves you and others. Think how this ends for you or others. Put a tick mark in one quadrant and proceed to read on about the four categories of activity.

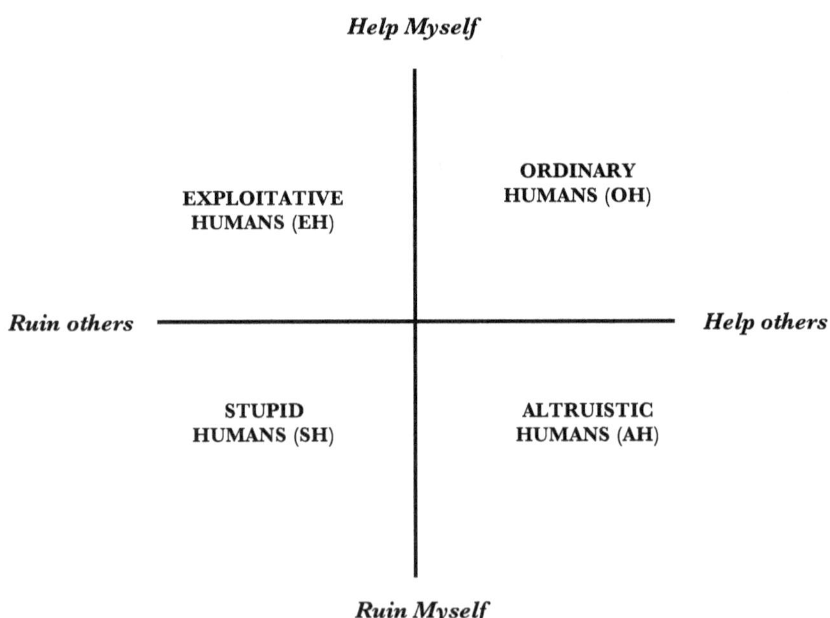

(Diagram by M.K. Turumella; image derived from Bhagavad Gita (4.13) "Four divisions are created based on the action and intentions behind those actions.") *(Internet Archive, 2017)[2]*

ORDINARY HUMANS (OH)

Suppose you are undertaking the activity of opening a business. If the result will be profitable to yourself and others also gain something from it, then put a tick mark in the quadrant – 'Help myself' and 'Help others'. This quadrant is labelled as Ordinary Humans (OH).

EXPLOITATIVE HUMANS (EH)

If you are starting an activity that results in your profit but ruins someone else, then put a tick in the left-hand topside of the quadrant – 'Help myself' and 'Ruin others'. Fraudulent and exploitative actions result in destroying others. The others do not know that your actions will ruin them, but only you know! This quadrant is labelled as Exploitative Humans (EH).

For example, the activity of the CFO of the collapsed Enron energy business falls into this quadrant. His action resulted in him living a wealthy lifestyle for nearly the whole of his life but resulted in the collapse of ENRON, ruining the lives of thousands of Enron employees and investors.

STUPID HUMANS (SH)

If your activity will ultimately ruin you and others, then put a tick in the quadrant on the bottom left – 'Ruin myself' and 'Ruin others'. This quadrant is labelled as 'Stupid Humans' (SH).

For example, the activity of the infamous fraud financier Bernie Madoff falls into this quadrant. He made vast amounts of money for himself and lived a lavish lifestyle, but in the end he died in jail and both his children died in tragic circumstances. His wife became homeless. He ruined himself, his family, and the lives of thousands who trusted him. And this is stupidity.

ALTRUISTIC HUMANS (AH)

If your activity will ruin you but help others, then put a tick in the bottom right-side quadrant, 'Ruin myself' and 'Help others'. This quadrant is labelled as 'Altruist Humans' (AH). If you are doing a donation or charity activity, also put a tick in this quadrant. Because though it is rare that someone gets ruined by doing charity, I know individuals who gave up all they have for charity. And this is altruism. For example, the activities undertaken by Abraham Lincoln, Martin Luther King and many activists fall into this quadrant. They know the activity they are undertaking is risky. They sacrificed their lives, but their actions did help others. Martin Luther King was assassinated, but his activity eventually saw Barack Obama getting elected as a President of the United States of America, and many black Americans ascended to the highest positions with dignity, respect and pride.

I encourage you to use the four quadrants of the human activity diagram and to do the four quadrants exercise every time you undertake any activity or perform an important action, because it gives us insight and clarity.

WE THE HUMANS

Nothing exists as a governance process without a human driving, empowering and validating it. The four quadrants diagram of human activity helps us identify who we are. Based on the **intention** behind the actions we are undertaking, we can identify ourselves as:

1. Ordinary Humans (OH)

2. Exploitative Humans (EH)

3. Altruist Humans (AH)

4. Stupid Humans (SH)

Each human action is intention-based. So, based on the activity, humans as agents can put themselves in one of these four quadrants and find out which type of human their action will make them be:

1. 'Help myself and help others' type of activities make us Ordinary Humans

2. 'Help myself and ruin others' type of activities make us Exploitative Humans

3. 'Ruin myself and also ruin others' type of activities makes us not-so-bright (stupid) Humans

4. 'Ruin myself but help others' type of activities make us Altruist Humans

Most of the human population are ordinary humans. They engage in activities where they gain, but others also gain. They share this earth with mutual respect and intend to give and take. Our world financial systems operate based on the intention that we trust and barter the correct exchange value.

The world of the wealthiest people, however, is made up of exploitative humans. This observation is not against people becoming wealthy. Still, the bitter truth is that some element of exploitation is involved in getting rich. Colonial governments were full of exploitative humans. All wars get started by exploitative humans. Any activity where any parties involved are deprived of the actual value they deserve by participating in such activity is exploitation.

Sure, one can walk away from getting exploited. Still, the prevailing personal economic conditions often make ordinary humans compromise with their exploitative fellow humans. For example, African farmers selling their produce for a lower price than they deserve is exploitation. But the farmer, desperate to make whatever little they can from their perishable produce, allows the buyer to bargain. Here the buyer who is bargaining down the price is the exploitative human. He may not think of his activity that way. But his action does give rise to inequality.

Humans get divided into these four quadrants based on their activities; therefore, no human is permanently fixed in one quadrant. For example, many wealthy people do give huge donations! And that activity puts them temporarily in the Altruist Human quadrant. Therefore our approach should be more towards understanding than being judgemental about people. The four-quadrant exercise is intended for self-reflection and introspection.

Altruist humans are always a rare species. Stupid humans exist, but I am not sure how many of our eight billion global population undertake stupid activities.

This book is about making ordinary and altruistic humans aware so they do not get hurt by the activities of exploitative and stupid humans. We want the people on the right-hand side of the diagram to be vigilant of the activities on the left-hand side.

People who engage in activities that fall on the right side of the four quadrants of the human activity diagram tend to get attacked and put in trouble by those who engage in the activities that fall on the left side of the diagram. The current imbalance, conflicts, refugee crisis, and immigration are all caused by a rift between the Modes of Action left and right. What an irony: people getting attacked for doing the right thing.

Exploitative and stupid humans cause ninety-nine per cent of all global calamities. The global climate crisis is the direct result of exploitative and foolish actions.

We humans have collective amnesia. We do not recognise that we are a part of this nature. We may be the highest in the predatory food chain. We may be the smartest of all species which inhabit the earth. But we forgot what it is to be human.

We know how to swim underwater by inventing scuba diving gear. We know how to fly by developing hang-gliders and aeroplanes to fly. If we see any obstacle, we create ways to surpass it. We know how to adapt to multiple situations, as if mimicking the behaviour of other species. But we forgot what it is to be human. We have forgotten our natural mode of being.

Instead of re-educating ourselves to live in harmony with the other species, we became arrogant. We adapted, twisted and abused technological and scientific advancements for our exploitation. But we forgot, which is where we have collective amnesia, that even dinosaurs were at the top of the predatory chain and also ruled this earth once upon a time, but are now extinct! We only see the fossils of their existence. The earth continued rotating even after the dinosaurs were gone. And the earth will rotate even if humans become extinct tomorrow due to our exploitative and stupid activities! We are nobody in the cosmos. We may attribute greater importance to ourselves due to our collective arrogance, but I'm afraid a day of reckoning will come when we may not get a chance to correct all our wrongs.

We must act while there is still time. We must pledge to stop all kinds of activities that lead to exploitation. There will not be a governor to prevent us from exploitation, and nor be a judge to jail us because we exploited the earth. No, the pledge to stop exploitation must come from each individual. It has to be voluntary, and there is no alternative. For example, people live in high-rise buildings, but rarely does anyone jump from them. Why? Because we all intrinsically know that jumping from height is suicidal and that the law of gravity governs our lives. In the same way, we all must arrive at an intrinsic recognition that exploitation is suicidal. It kills us all. And that we are all governed by invisible laws of nature. If we do not do the right thing and continue to cause imbalance, then Nature, the cosmos, will choose to correct our course. It would prefer to wipe us clean. The God of death knows no mercy! Therefore we must all voluntarily act and stop all our exploitative actions.

We are empathetic beings. Our gut feels our surroundings. We act based on our gut instincts. For example, if a small child is crying out alone on a street corner, most passersby would stop and enquire about the child's reason for crying. But we would not stop to enquire if the child is happy and playing. Why? Because our gut instinct tells us that being happy and content is a natural state of being, while being miserable is an imbalance. So we respond to the child's cry.

We do respond to correct the imbalance in our surroundings, society, and country we live in. Still, alas, we cannot respond to the inequality in the world because we are divided. We are selfishly acting as countries but not as a whole humanity. We cannot respond as a human species using our collective gut human instinct because we are divided. We made laws worldwide to cripple the voices of human intuition. We are restricted. Our hands are tied worldwide in all countries, by various draconian laws and customs.

I have encountered many situations where knowledgeable, most respected professionals have hesitated to voice their opinions. They are scared that they will lose their job if they say anything not seen in a good light by the rulers of their workspace, and instead walkon eggshells. Nearly everyone in human societies today appears to be scared of exploitative humans enforcing exploitative laws.

The question is, how did we humans reach this point?! Why should people who want to respond to the imbalances in their surroundings feel like they are walking on eggshells?! Do they have to risk their safety, security and finances to do the right thing? And this is the reason why we do not see many humans responding from the altruistic human quadrant in the four quadrants of the human activity diagram. Altruism is required to bring a change of heart in exploitative humans and their activities.

IMPACT OF EXPLOITATIONS AND FRAUDS

When mega-corporations like ENRON in America or Satyam Computers in India collapsed due to fraudulent activity at the top level, only the CEO, CFO and a handful of top executives got punished. And this is where today's governance systems are failing. They are designed in favour of exploitation. Take the case of ENRON, which employed nearly 37,000 people. Besides the C-level, a thousand or more senior executives were on very high salaries and dividends, and made millions when ENRON was at its height. The money earned was disproportionate to the money earned by the rest of the employees. The excessive salary and income from dividends justified saying they are clever individuals with leadership qualities. If this was correct, then why did they let ENRON fail? Suppose the answer is they did not see it coming. In that case, their intelligence is no better than any other salary-earning employee on minimum wages. So they did not justify their high earnings right from the beginning! Therefore, all high-paid executives should have had to voluntarily give up their earnings into the fund to protect the employees whose lives were ruined because of the collapse.

The exploitative situation I have explained using **ENRON** as an example is merely the tip of the iceberg. Corporate and government systems across the world are designed to exploit. Only a handful of top executives get punished when such corporations and governments fail. And in addition, many other top earners who supported them gained millions from supporting such exploitative activities. They walked away and retired in peace with the immense wealth they earned from participating in such exploitation. There is no fairness in such systems. They are not helpful for future human evolution.

Fraud is a stupid activity. One gets jailed for participating in such an activity. The fraudster initially makes the fraudulent action appear like a regular human activity. For example, imagine he is selling a home which he has no authority to sell. Other humans fall for it. They think they are participating in a genuine home-buying activity. But all frauds carry some telltale signatures. Humans are blessed with the gut feeling to recognise it. So if they express doubt, the fraudster makes his action appear generous. The fraudster uses all the cunning means available to cheat his victim. He tells his buyer that the home costs two million dollars in the market, but he will reduce the price in half because he likes the buyer. If the buyer believes him, then the fraudster has gained. He helped himself with a million dollars by ruining others. Till this point, it is an exploitative action. The damage to the innocent buyer is done. Until the law catches up with the fraudster, his action makes him remain in the exploitative human quadrant. After the fraudster gets convicted, his action moves into the stupidity quadrant.

Now imagine certain countries where corruption is rife, where police act as watchdogs for the corrupt. Fraudsters get away with their fraud, thus ruining the lives of innocent humans who engage in activities belonging to the ordinary human quadrant! In such countries where exploitation is the system, the defeated, the hurt, the disenfranchised, the hapless humans who are subjected to such ruthless exploitation dream of seeking life somewhere else, somewhere better, in another country. They leave the country where they are exploited to somewhere where they hope to have a better life. Because they have no means to make it to their destination country through legal channels, they attempt to reach their destination country illegally, and we call these exploited humans 'refugees'. Every refugee has a story to tell. But it all comes down to the four quadrants of activity. The bottom line is that the actions of exploitative and stupid humans have ruined people's lives and turned them into refugees.

But not all humans openly acknowledge that they are exploited. Many remain silent, and instead of putting up with the exploitation, immigrate using legally available channels. They eventually settle and take up citizenship in other countries.

Migration is never an answer to human misery because exploitation is everywhere around the globe. Some countries covertly cause exploitation and enjoy the riches gained from such covert exploitation.

What we are witnessing today and have done from time immemorial is that we humans are causing hurt, albeit unknowingly, to other humans by participating in exploitative activities, such as buying cloth that was made cheaply in another country. Don't we know that by looking to buy cheap, we are depriving a citizen of our own country of a job? World trade agreements are designed to protect everyone. But are they working?! Who is enforcing? What is the inner psychological makeup of the persons who are implementing?

Protectionism is not an answer to human misery. History tells us that countries which followed protective trade policies have deprived other countries of development. Therefore, the answer lies in borderless thinking.

How will our policies shape up if we collapse all human-drawn borders and act as one earth with no central government but governed by each capable human living anywhere on earth? It means all knowledge available to any government, thus far anywhere in the world, must be open to the individual.

If any single human participates in exploitative action, there will be suffering in this world. The answer to the suffering is that humans must stop exploiting each other. From micro to macro, we have built the world economy based on exploitation in the past. Now some countries continue to engage in exploitation to retain their superior position.

Some countries exploit other countries for human resources, oil, gold, and other reasons. Such actions eventually lead to the breakdown of harmonious natural human existence in the exploited country, leading to crises, and revolutions in the country, culminating in refugee crisis. I discuss this further in the chapter, 'The four quadrants of governance and policy structures'.

I have named this book *Humans without Borders* to point out that we are a single humanity living in artificially drawn borders, governed by specific laws and ruled by certain people. In some countries, some of these laws were designed in the colonial past with a sinister aim to rule ruthlessly and exploit. And this is the reason why many colonised nations remain in abject poverty even today.

All humanity must come together to walk towards an age of enlightenment where we can feel free to act, as free as a whale which travels thousands of miles around the world unrestricted and unexploited. We must feel free to act like birds which fly thousands of miles unexploited, living their natural life.

In today's world, we have borderless whales and birds but we do not have borderless humans. The reason is that we humans are engaged in exploitative actions. Warmongers with muscle and manpower subdued the rest of the population. The forces of exploitation drew borders and confined humans within these borders. So humans have to search for their food, for their living and for their protection within these borders.

And the model of confining oneself to a single country and acting with patriotism only towards that country is not working. Some nations on this earth can offer nothing to their citizens. So what do the citizens do? They try to migrate. Let us suppose all the citizens migrate. Then what happens to the existence of the country?

We must recognise that it is people who give existence to any nation, not artificially drawn borders. In ancient times people existed as tribes. Their group bonds were thick, and they carried their tribal identity and culture. But wars destroyed these cultures. Religion and its belief structures influence culture, but culture is not religion.

Culture continues even after the religious beliefs of the people change.

All wars are acts of violent exploitation. The world has witnessed so many wars during this century alone. Many trade agreements lead to exploitation. They make agreements with autocratic countries that do not share their wealth with the citizens or give their citizens the necessary freedom. But trade agreements ignore the suffering of ordinary citizens, and that results in revolt, which is why we have witnessed so many revolutions. The revolutions in the Middle East of the early 2010s called the Arab Spring are an example.

Some religions have also become exploitative. Whether the founder of those religions intended it that way or not, humans started using religious activities to exploit the vulnerable. There used to be numerous tribes, with identities and cultures worldwide and at least 200 religions identified as practised by these ancient humans. But today, we only see five major religions influencing the world. They are Christianity, Islam, Judaism, Hindu ism and Buddhism. What happened to the rest? They were all extinguished by exploitative humans through wars, by creating artificial scarcity of resources and by subjugation. There are a few other minor religions existing today but we do not see them influencing the world to the same degree.

We humans are destroying the world with our exploitative activities. But fortunately, there is a great intention to protect the world from exploitation. For example, everyone has a right to life. To achieve this human right, to enshrine it as a global human rights charter, and to make all countries sign up, was the result of altruist humans blessed by wisdom acting as true leaders of humanity. The altruism is still there, and the good intention to protect the world and the vulnerable is still there. But it is time to take it to the next level. We must progress towards Borderless Humanity.

Only Humans without Borders can see the world as a single globe, seeing the oneness of humanity and acting in the interest of humanity. It is impossible to think in oneness as long as we are divided into many countries with artificial borders. But is it possible? Can we create a single humanity capable of self-regulating its activities? Can we enable each adult human to make informed decisions?!

Can we aim to provide the maximum amount of peace, love and prosperity to the maximum number of people in the world?

WE GET JUDGEMENTAL

We humans come with our flaws. There is no perfect human. Yet we get very judgemental when we see faults in others.

Exploitative and stupid humans tend to be highly judgemental. Because they can exploit by judging; for example, look at the people who engage in blackmailing activities or those who shame others for their weaknesses. There is an element of exploitation in all sorts of judgmental attitudes.

In the case of stupid humans, they are not exploitative because they initially think they are super-bright by exploiting, even though, it results in the ruin of all. We cannot address human stupidity without ring-fencing the impact. Humans inevitably do stupid things. So we must concentrate on reducing the impact of such foolish actions.

2

HUMAN NATURE

Where the mind is without fear and the head is held high;
Where knowledge is free;
Where the world has not been broken up into fragments by
narrow domestic walls;
Where words come out from the depth of truth;
Where tireless striving stretches its arms towards perfection;
Where the clear stream of reason has not lost its way into the
dreary desert sand
of dead habit;
Where the mind is led forward by thee into ever-widening
thought and action
Into that heaven of freedom, my Father, let my country
awake.

'Gitanjali 35', from *Gitanjali*, 1912,
by Dr Rabindranath Tagore (Tagore, n.d., pp.70–71)[3]

It is essential to understand the nature of humans to know why any human undertakes any action that falls in one of the four quadrants of human activity. We humans operate in this world with a notion of self, identified as the ego, which makes us express 'I am this, I want this, I do this', etc. The I, the ego, transacts in this world with three awareness levels and strives to fulfil three primal desires.

THREE LEVELS OF AWARENESS

Every day, all humans participate in some exploitative human activity, all participate in ordinary human activity, all participate in altruistic human activity, and all participate in stupid activities. But how long they continue these activities or withdraw and self-regulate is based on their inner psychological make-up, the level of their knowledge towards the activity, and how much they get pressured into participating in it.

Recognising that three levels of awareness influence all our actions is essential.

The Three Levels of Human Awareness

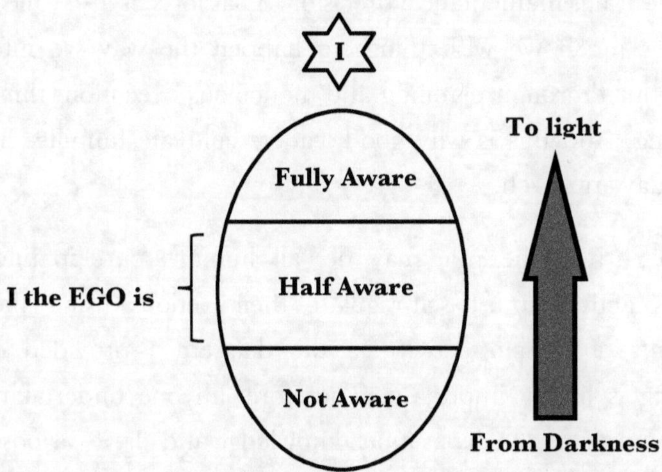

(Diagram by M.K. Turumella; image derived from the commentary on the Bṛhadāraṇyaka Upaniṣad (1.3.28.) by Adi Shankara [4], 'The Cosmic Egg' in the Brahmanda Purana (1.1.1.43-44) [5], egg diagram inspiration from Psychosynthesis and Act of Will by Dr Roberto Assagioli, 1888) (Assagioli, n.d., p.15) [6]

FULLY AWARE / UNDERSTANDING

Before undertaking any activity, one must know what one is trying to achieve, why it is necessary, what material instruments are available to achieve it and who will help. For example, when starting a new business venture, we must have a business plan. Why is it we want to do this business? What instruments are available to do business, such as office space, equipment, etc.? Who is going to help us in this business? Suppliers, buyers, business partners and shareholders. Having thorough knowledge and help from suppliers, buyers, business partners, and shareholders will drive the business 80% towards success. Only GOD has control over the remaining 20%.

There is an overwhelming governing force that has control over this universe. It has mathematical precision. That force is also called God. However much we wish things to happen the way we intended, despite our thorough planning and meticulous execution, things can go wrong! And this is why good leaders cultivate humility in their day-to-day approach.

However trivial the role may be, all humans participating in a business activity must self-regulate their actions using the four quadrants of human activity in the diagram I provided earlier. Knowing is highly important. Therefore, anyone undertaking any activity must strive to get as much knowledge and clarity as possible.

Knowledge at this level is compared to walking in bright daylight. Everything is visible, and one can stay clear of any obstacles.

Most people want to do the right thing, but how will they know what's right, unless full knowledge and consequences of undertaking an action are within their reach? Exploitative humans use this knowledge gap as a noose to trap others. They trap ordinary people. By denying them the proper knowledge, they gain for themselves and ruin others through their exploitative actions.

For example, a CFO of a 17,000-employee company was doing fraudulent accounting. But he alone has the knowledge that he is committing fraud. The remaining 17,000 employees or company shareholders do not know that fraud is occurring. Otherwise, why would they let him commit fraud? Thus, by denying the proper knowledge to the people involved, the exploitative CFO has created a noose, a trap for his gain. When the scam is discovered, the consequences fall on the good 17,000 people who lose their jobs, and the investors see their wealth evaporate.

The psychological consequences of losing one's job are devastating for many. After working for nearly thirty years in the corporate world and having worked for many companies, I know the disastrous consequences people experience when lose their job. Many people identify their worth with the job that they do. Employment gives them confidence. It gives them an identity. This is one of the reasons why the police, the military and other professionals wear uniforms that give them pride in their work.

When people lose their employment, they lose confidence. Some never fully recover from the psychological trauma of losing their job. Therefore, one must try to get as much knowledge as possible to stay safe from exploitation. Knowledge is the key to avoiding many miseries. Knowledge and truth set one free from exploitation. Expanding one's knowledge horizon is one of the best ways to remain confident in life. Picking up other job skills, staying informed about current trends, being adaptable to change and having a flexible mindset are excellent strategies for facing the trauma any sudden loss may cause.

A business person's mode of action must be 'I am helping myself by doing or participating in this business, but I am also helping others'. For a worker, commitment to work is essential. People must aim to do ordinary or philanthropic activities. They must resist the temptation to participate in exploitation and must beware of human stupidity.

There are two paths to living life in this world - the path of perseverance and the crooked path. The path of perseverance is arduous in the beginning. People who travel this path face a lot of obstacles. But it gets easy as they endure all the pain and continue to walk this life path. The path becomes easy and gives them lasting peace and also riches. For example, students study hard to enter their chosen professions. They find it difficult during their study because they have to manage their meagre finances, take care of their daily life, and study hard. But in the end, they succeed and enjoy professional life. Those who join jobs at an entry-level work diligently and slowly rise to the company's top positions. It is a slow path. It is difficult initially, but those who travel it find peace and contentment …

Whereas some people want to get rich quickly! There is nothing wrong with having ambition. But the path some of them chose to get rich quickly is the path of the crooked. It gives very high gains in the beginning, and appears that people who are walking this path are lucky due to the wealth they enjoy, but as they walk through the path of life, they start feeling misery, finally leading them to disaster. Fraudsters, cheaters, corrupt and greedy people walk the path of crooked. They go for quick gains. These people appear to enjoy life, but in the end, they get jailed and die miserable due to the misery they have caused other people.

Knowledge, or the highest level of awareness, is a great enabler to help us understand our path in life.

HALF AWARE / MISUNDERSTANDING

The next level of awareness is called being half-aware. This is the most dangerous mental state. It causes confusion. People who have half-knowledge suffer from a trust deficit. They act with suspicion towards everything. Most evil dictators are people with half-knowledge. Half-knowledge is the mother of all misunderstandings.

And nearly all conflicts in this world are caused due to misunderstandings.

Any endeavour undertaken with half-knowledge will result in calamity. Misunderstanding is a pathway to chaos. It can be compared to someone who does not know how to swim and also does not know the depth of the river they are trying to swim across. The river could be only a foot deep, or it could be too deep to stand in. Taking a chance in such a situation is too risky. Yet some do choose the risk. Those who choose the risk, but do not learn on their way, fail. But those who succeed keep learning as they progress. Life is an everyday learning process for those who are successful in life. We all start from ignorance, gain half-knowledge during the process and become fully knowledgeable after gaining experience.

However, we must recognise that half-knowledge or being half-aware is perilous for any human to operate. Think how often we make erroneous decisions because we are only half aware of the situation. In the criminal justice system, think how many innocents were incarcerated for life because someone up there in the chain of authority were so over-confident strongly in their own investigative skills that they overlooked crucial or circumstantial evidence that may have opened up other possibilities.

Half-knowledge is compared to being in a state of twilight. Imagine you are walking alone in the wilderness, and it is twilight. In the twilight, we cannot see things clearly. Imagine seeing something you thought was a snake in the twilight. The thought frightens you,.. so you take a stick and strike to kill it. The snake was not moving even after you hit it; perhaps, it was dead already. To confirm your assumption, you switch on a torch and realise in that light that it was never a snake but a rope… The misunderstanding caused you a lot of mental agony and you exerted a lot of mental energy I beating up that imaginary snake. You could have avoided all this had you used the torch right from the beginning. Unfortunately, not all humans are blessed with that kind of brightness, and in life, many of us do things without using the help of the light of knowledge.

Not all humans are blessed with the intellectual capacity to understand everything. The remedy to it is team-building. Either we become a part of a team where the team lead is more knowledgeable and a subject-matter expert, or we become the leads but recruit those with the right skills. Either way, humans can compensate for what we lack by forming a tactical life bond with others who have what we do not have. But this creates a problem! In the eagerness to compensate for the skills which they do not have, humans who submit their personal power to the team leader risk the chance of being exploited...

On the contrary, if we lead the team by blindly trusting the augmenting skills of other people we recruit, it could lead to disaster, ruining us and everyone else in the group – leading us to fall into the stupidity quadrant. I noticed that many failed leaders fail because they do not know how to balance power. They must learn how to strike the right balance.

Half-knowledge is dangerous. Humans tend to compensate for unknown facts with assumptions that lead to disastrous conclusions. Therefore, knowing the unknowns and acknowledging the consequences help us avoid causing problems to our fellow humans, other species, the environment and the Earth.

NOT AWARE / IGNORANCE

Ignorance is like total darkness. It is the absence of knowledge and the beginning of our life's journey. We all start our life's journey as ignorants. Our life is nothing but a journey from darkness to light. Ignorance is the mental inability to comprehend a given situation. For example, a person may be frightened of snakes. But when that person is walking in total darkness, he will not get scared even if he crosses paths with a most venomous snake. Because it was dark and he did not see the snake!

Any action undertaken in Ignorance is dangerous because it can lead to fatal consequences. Stupid people undertake activities while ignorant, which is why they ruin themselves and others due to their actions. Ignorance gives temporary bliss and permanent pain. Therefore one must be aware of the level of ignorance one has and self-regulate. Strive to get out of ignorance. If it gets impossible to get out of ignorance, then accept it as a challenge and regulate life so that we do not cause pain to others.

EXPLOITATION AND LEVELS OF AWARENESS

Exploitative humans use the level of awareness in others to exploit them. A fully aware person rarely gets influenced. It is only the half-aware or not aware or ignorant people who fall prey to exploitation. Denial of the correct information, keeping people in the dark, or spreading false information is the age-old tactic of exploitative individuals.

The sad part is that exploitative governments keep people in darkness by denying them information. In such situations, the state becomes the persecutor, and they willingly ignore the plight of their subjects. Therefore, the best answer to many problems is to make the maximum number of people aware. Keeping secrets from one another is a strategy used solely for exploitation.

Truth is compelling. And truth has many dimensions. Each human must be able to arrive at the truth independently. Making truth widespread and fully available for all humans is one way to achieve global peace.

THREE PRIMAL DESIRES

Now that we know that our inner makeup has three levels of awareness and that our awareness level decides our journey in life, let us try to understand what prompts all our actions. What exactly motivates us to act in this world? Why do we do what we do?

We act in this world because we are driven by three extremely powerful primal desires. We are driven by these three. All activities in our day-to-day life are tied to fulfilling one of these three. Please see the diagram below:

Triangle of the Three Primal Human Desires

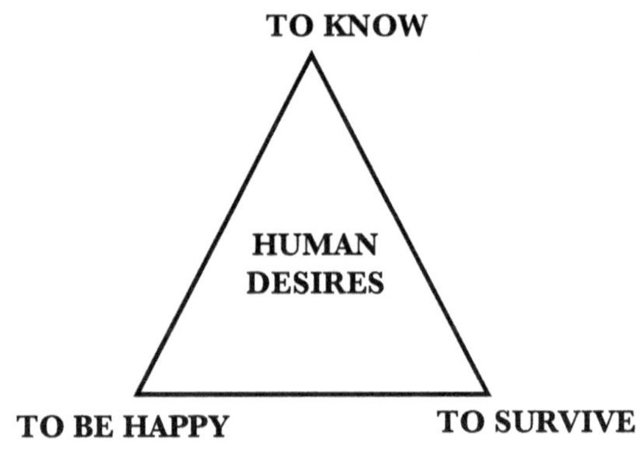

(Diagram by M.K. Turumella; inspired by Upanishads and commentary on Brahmasutras by Sri Adi Shankara)

We humans have three desires which propel our life in all sorts of directions. We want **to know**, we want **to survive**, and we want **to be happy**. We seek these three throughout our human life.

1. We want permanent happiness.
2. We want immortality. We want to live forever.
3. We want to acquire all knowledge.

Our life is driven by seeking these three. Any deficiency in fulfilling these three makes us unstable, unhappy and mentally ill. We are in conflict when what we seek is denied to us. There are no exceptions to this desire triangle. Refer to the four quadrants of the human activity diagram. Why do we act at all? Our soul gets restless because it is always powerfully drawn towards fulfilling these three desires.

WE SEEK KNOWLEDGE

We are born with an urge to acquire knowledge. As infants, we get attracted to bright objects and put them in our mouths because we want to know. Our five sense organs – the eyes, ears, nose, tongue and skin – assist us in acquiring knowledge.

For example, think of why you read this book. It is to fulfil a desire in you to know.

Incredible illusions happen when the five sense organs get deceived by clever means. Therefore Ignorance is also a kind of knowledge that exploitative forces cleverly harvest for their gains. Exploitative individuals worldwide use laws that allow us or deny us what we seek.

WE WANT TO SURVIVE

We are driven by a powerful urge to survive. Though nobody has escaped the inevitable jaws of death, we are frightened of death. In time, everyone every living thing dies. But we have a default switch inside us. By default, we desire to live. Imagine a person finds a snake in his bedroom. He would not rest until the snake gets captured or killed because that snake has threatened the survival instinct of that person. The snake has to die so that he can survive. All strategies are energised based on the desire to survive.

Why do we eat or drink? Because we know if we do not eat or drink, we will not survive. Therefore to fulfil a desire to survive, we eat and drink.

Each individual is born with this instinct to survive. We team up if the threat exceeds an individual's capacity to survive. We become a tribe to face a threat to survival collectively.

We humans acquire lethal instruments such as guns because we want to survive. Acquiring arms is one of the strategies to survive. All countries maintain militaries because they intend to prevail. A military is nothing but an expression of the survival instinct of the total population of that country. Exploitative individuals can cleverly use this to their advantage.

Exploitative humans create false threats and create grand illusions to appeal to the survival instinct in humans strategically. For example, when the Iraq war was waged, most citizens cooperated because their governments told them that Iraq had Weapons of Mass Destruction (WMD). This means there was a severe threat to our survival. Therefore go to war and remove the threat. But in hindsight, we know now that the WMD was a lie. But why lie? I do not think democratic governments wilfully lie because the legislators know they have to go to elections. Therefore, one of the humans or a group up in the chain of command had created a false report for whatever reasons, and the rulers fell hook, line and sinker. Such activity, which gives gains to some and ruins others, falls into the exploitative human quadrant in our Four Quadrants of Human Activity diagram. But in some countries, rulers may have lied to their citizens; we do not know. But to exploit what the forces in government lied to their citizens is questionable.

Suffice it to say, our desire to survive makes us put innocent lives in danger, destroy their natural habitat and make refugees out of them. Our desire to survive is putting the planet at risk. Which means we are destroying the very same earth which helps us survive.

WE WANT TO BE HAPPY

We have a powerful desire to be happy. Why do you go to a concert, watch a movie, meet friends and family, and go on vacations? It is to fulfil the desire to be happy. We all want to be happy. But because happiness is subjective, we can not expect others to be happy in our happiness. For example, someone loves drinking bourbon. He feels delighted if anyone offers him a bottle of bourbon. But another person hates alcohol. Any sight of a bottle of bourbon makes him feel totally unhappy. The same bottle of bourbon causes happiness in one human and unhappiness in another. Therefore happiness is not in the material object but in the subject's mind. This means material things do not give any satisfaction. Contemplating this truth of life will provide us with contentment. It helps us to withstand the storms which cause us sadness.

Exploitative individuals commoditise happiness. They provide or deny us happiness. There will be someone ready to exploit as long as our desire to be happy depends on others!

WE ARE TRIANGLES WITH SHARP EDGES

You may be wondering why Triangle. In Hindu religious texts, Triangle is called Trikona. Tri means Three, and Kona means angles. It is the strongest shape. Any weight placed on a triangle is evenly distributed on all three. The three powerful desires in the human hold the person together and propel the person to progress in the journey called life. A person disintegrates and suffers psychologically if the three powerful desires are not holding him up. That is why in Sri Sukta of *Rigveda* and Sri Chakra Yantra[7] in *Tantra*, the world and its mysterious capability to cause profound delusion called Maya is depicted using Triangles.

Each and every human action is driven by these three desires. These desires are so profound that they force us to join or build a team, compel us to form a group and make us a tribe.

We humans are a single species. We are a homogeneous mass of consciousness. However, our three desires in an unfulfilled state do not allow us to achieve that wholeness with our kind. We are constantly endeavouring to fulfil the three desires. As our three desires reach their specific individualistic optimally fulfilled state, we feel whole and we expand! We expand by merging with fellow humans, fellow beings, and nature. The merging becomes automatic. It is recognisable through our love, sacrifice, altruism and non-violent attitude at all levels of our human expression. In such a state of expansion, we become a circle everywhere with a circumference of nowhere. There is no reason for conflict in such an expansion.

So what is stopping us from evolving into that penultimate state of oneness? We humans have become our own obstacles. Instead of moving as smooth-edged circles which cause no harm to each even while separated, we prefer to remain as three-pointed triangles that pierce and violently hurt each other.

Imagine someone desires to know about something which another human knows better. the one who does not know seeks knowledge transfer from the one who knows. They are like two triangles —. one who knows and the other who does not know. Imagine the knowledge transfer is denied! They act like extremely pointed, sharp-edged triangles with lethal capabilities. The one who knows will violently harm the other to deny them the knowledge they themselves hold, and the other one will find to get hold of the knowledge they lack. They fight … The same is the case with happiness. If one human denies another happiness, then they fight. This is also the case with survival. If one human threatens the survival of the other, they fight! Whether we consciously recognise it or not as triangles, we are constantly engaged in a fight.

On the contrary, if the person who has knowledge *agrees* to the knowledge transfer, then due to the understanding between these two individuals, a psychological merging happens! Knowledge flows from one to the other. In some cases, they team up and act as a single circle. The person with knowledge augments the capability of the one who does not know. Thus they team up to survive and be happy in their learning.

EGO IS THE KING

The three primal desires – to know, be happy and survive– which I mentioned above, all revolve around I, the first person singular. This 'I', also called 'the ego', gives a distinctive identity to the individual. In a totally fulfilled state, it knows, it survives, and it is happy. But in an unfulfilled state, it does not know; and is scared because it feels its survival is doubtful. Human life is an informed but involuntary swinging between fulfilled and unfulfilled states. The ego feels depressed when it feels it is in an unfulfilled state., and feels elated when it feels it is in a fulfilled state. But because it is in an involuntary swing, it has no control over what it feels; so it keeps swinging between fulfilled and unfulfilled states.

The most significant problem an ego faces is when it does not have a measurement, when it does not know how much knowledge is enough or how much safety is enough or how much happiness is enough. This 'enough' state is called contentment. The ego faces problems when it does not feel contented.

A healthy ego knows how much it does not know, where it is not happy and when its existence is under threat. A healthy human ego can set boundaries for its knowledge, happiness, and survival. It operates within these boundaries and leads an informed and carefully executed life from the womb to the tomb, from its birth to its death!

One way a healthy human ego is formed is through proper education. Education helps develop the capability in the mind of proper logic and proper discrimination, such that a healthy mind can discriminate between right and wrong actions. Only a healthy human ego can grasp those choices and do the right thing. There are many tools a healthy human ego can use to make an informed choice between right and wrong. The four quadrants of the human activity diagram, which I illustrated earlier, is one such tool.

What do I mean by education helping develop proper logic? Logic helps people to become content. An interesting story explains this. A teacher who is teaching the logic of contentment to his students gives a diamond to a student and asks them to keep it safely till the evening. The student is conscientious and protects it, but by the evening, the diamond has disappeared. The student has lost it. He starts crying bitterly because he knows the teacher will scold him for losing the diamond. So the student goes to the teacher crying.

'Sir, I lost the diamond', cries the student.

'Oh, you lost it! What made you cry?' asks the teacher.

'Sir, I am crying because I lost the diamond' the student replies.

'Why were you not crying this morning?' asks the teacher.

Bewildered at the question the teacher is asking, the student replies 'Sir, I had no reason to cry because I had the diamond with me'.

Then the teacher consoled the student in this way:

'Oh child, you had the diamond in the morning but lost it by the evening. You are crying because you were in possession of a precious diamond, and you lost it. If you had never possessed the precious diamond, you would never cry. Yesterday evening, the diamond was with me. You have no memory of its existence. But this morning, after I gave it to you, you got the memory of it. You lost the diamond by the evening, and though you physically lost the diamond, you never lost the memory of it. And it is the memory of this precious diamond which is making you cry! Now think about when that memory entered you and why it is making you cry. One cannot grieve for something one has never had. '

The aim of the teacher was not the diamond. But, using the diamond, the teacher wanted to teach the student the nature of fulfilled and unfulfilled states of mind.

Humans search for happiness because logically, at one point in time, they know what it is to be happy! One must have had the happiness to feel sorrow because he lost it. One must be happy, immortal and omniscient, but one has fallen down from that state of totality. A human feels unhappy because he feels he is in such a fallen state. The ego is the one which can get a proper education. With proper education, the ego can apply logic and feel contented. Karma is one of the logics taught to the seekers to feel contented and take control.

Unfortunately, in some individuals, the ego does not develop in a healthy state. Especially children who face trauma at a very early stage of life tend to get into trouble because their ego is not adequately formed. Therefore children from traumatic households struggle to set boundaries for themselves. When the ego does not know its boundaries, then it becomes unhealthy. It becomes exploitative. It also acts stupidly. During this unhealthy process, It becomes toxic for others!

In a state of toxicity, the ego acts like a mad king. It ruthlessly gives 'off with its head' commands to whomever it likes or dislikes. This state of misaligned boundaries gives rise to a very toxic emotion called 'cognitive dissonance'.

While travelling through the journey of life from womb to tomb, the ego undergoes many emotions. Six of them are very interesting and worth knowing. They are desire, cognitive dissonance, greed, delusion, arrogance and jealousy. These emotions follow an interesting pattern. They start with desire, and desire turns into the cognitive dissonance that turns into greed then greed deludes the person. A person in delusion becomes arrogant, and an arrogant person feels jealous of others. I already explained that desire is the seed in each person and acts as a triangle to know, be happy and survive. Nothing is wrong with desire, but unregulated or unintelligent desire gives rise to a destructive emotion called Cognitive Dissonance. Any person who undergoes this cognitive dissonance has a high chance of becoming either exploitative or stupid.

COGNITIVE DISSONANCE

In simple terms the uncontrollable uneasiness or mental propulsion one feels to set something to how that person wishes to see it is cognitive dissonance.

For example, let us imagine you park regularly at a particular spot. Though you do not own that parking spot, you find it is quite convenient for you. The desire in you to find that spot vacant is very strong. But one day you find someone else trying to park in that space. You get upset and approach that driver asking them to move their car because you park there. The driver replies it is a community parking space therefore he has every right to park there. You feel so enraged you do everything in your capacity to argue, bully and fight with that person till you find that driver move away fearing your rage! That rage is cognitive dissonance.

As per *Bhagawad Gita* (2.62), cognitive dissonance starts with a strong desire[8]. Then the desire turns into emotional symbiosis, where the person develops near identification with their desired state. The person fails to distinguish between the emotional energy of their personal self and the energy evoked by their object of desire. When the object of their desire is criticised, they feel they have been cut off from the symbiosis, like an infant cut from his mother's umbilical cord! An infant cries helplessly, but in a grown person, the feeling of helplessness turns into cognitive dissonance, . a highly destructive state often with fatal consequences. No person is immune to this.

For example, imagine a person taught from childhood about the greatness of his prophet. He develops a desire in which he sees his prophet as infallible. Slowly the energy of this constant desire welds the energy of his ego with the energy developed through the external inputs praising his prophet. Thus the emotional energies of the person and prophet become one. Therefore, when anyone criticises his prophet, the person who worships his prophet feels severe dissonance; we usually call this anger, but this cognitive dissonance state is beyond anger. It is rage. It feels like the death of an ego. A healthy human can reflect their inner rage and hold a healthy debate with the criticising human. But an unhealthy human may not be able to process those thoughts and feelings due to many factors, such as childhood trauma or the trauma inflicted upon them as an immigrant refugee. Thus, the only way they feel during that rage induced by cognitive dissonance is to destroy any object causing dissonance until they return to consonance. A gun in the hands of such a destructive person can destroy the whole world!

For example, in France, a gunman massacred Charlie Hebdo cartoonists because he was undergoing cognitive dissonance. We can find many examples of cognitive dissonance. People who undergo road rage are suffering from cognitive dissonance.

(Cognitive dissonance is discussed more fully in a later chapter because it requires serious attention.)

THE NATURE OF KARMA

There are two overwhelming forces which govern this universe. They are gravity and karma. We are all familiar with gravity. It is scientifically very well explained. But karma is not that well explained because the word is used more in religious and philosophical discourses.

Gravity is the force which binds physical matter. We are all walking on this earth because of gravity. An apple from a tree falls to the ground because of gravity. The sun, the moon, the planets, the stars, the whole physical matter of galaxies is bound together because of this invisible force called gravity.

But then the question arises of what makes one recognise the force of gravity? The rotation of the moon? The gentle touch of a passing breeze? The beautiful fragrance of a flower? The serene sound of a gentle stream? What makes one tremble in fear? What makes one laugh out loud? All these are expressions of consciousness. Consciousness is the state of being aware. Consciousness enables us to respond to our surroundings. Consciousness is the alive principle. I think, I write, I read, I listen; all this is only possible because I am conscious. I am alive. But we all know that the state of being alive is time-bound. We are all born in time and die at some point in time.

Humans are thought to have a maximum of some hundred years of life, while elephants can live up to 70 years and mayflies have a lifespan of only a few hours or a day. What force decides how long something lives, what one feels, what one eats, drinks, etc.? The force is called Karma.

Gravity binds the physically visible matter. At the same time, Karma binds the consciousness to physical matter. A person who accidentally falls from the tenth floor of a building inevitably gets hurt. In the same way, any being who is conscious, who thinks, eats, drinks, walks or flies, inevitably gets hurt. Just as one takes every precaution not to fall from the tenth floor of a building, one must take every precaution not to get hurt while living in this universe consciously. The philosophical lessons about karma help us understand how to deal with this universe while we are alive. Humans have the unique capability to live in harmony with our karma.

THE FOUR URGES

We are hardwired with four animalistic urges: food, sleep, sex and fear. Other animals also have these four urges. Please see the following illustration of how these four fit in the triangle of three desires.

Four urges and triangle of human desires, by M.K. Turumella

We seek food to survive. We fear danger because we want to survive. The feeling of fear helps us to avoid threats and feel safe. We want to have sex for two reasons: to feel happy and to survive the species through procreation. We sleep because we want to relax and feel happy. We want to know. To acquire knowledge, we meet people, make friends to know where to get good food, gather sexual partners, where to sleep, and how to avoid danger etc.

Thus far, almost all laws that human societies have created focus on providing and regulating these four things: food, sex, sleep and safety. Now you may wonder what the relation is between exploitation and these four urges! Humans go mad when deprived of food, sex, sleep and safety. Exploitative humans use these four to trap, to enslave! For thousands of years, exploitative forces have weaponised these four urges. I explain weaponisation in a separate chapter.

CUNNING STRATEGIES

We become highly selfish when we forget that we are a part of humanity. Greed is the senseless pursuit of the three desires while denying the equal right of others to fulfil these three desires. Any action we undertake, while we are selfish or greedy, makes us fall into the exploitative or stupid human quadrant in the Four Quadrants of Human Activity diagram. The human with knowledge also seeks to survive and be happy. But conflict starts when he denies that to the others. There will be violence between triangles. They keep fighting, refuting each other chances to survive and to be happy. Eventually, the strongest triangle succeeds and metamorphoses into a circle of harmless edges.

This is how we humans are engaged in this world. As a whole, we want to be like circles but as primitives we act like triangles. We created countries, drew artificial borders and started fighting with each other!

WHY WE CLASH

Evolution made us social animals. We seek to live in societies to fulfil our three shared desires: to know, be happy, and survive. We learned to live in communities by compromising with each other. An emotion called gratitude is used to bind us in shared understanding. The more gratitude we cultivate in our hearts, the more humble we become.

Unfortunately, nowadays societies have become structures of convenience. Neighbours who live next door do not know each other. Gratitude is delinked by the top-down structure of governments. As a result, people who live in societies of convenience only seek to demand their rights, rather than showing any eagerness to fulfil their responsibilities. And highly selfish, exploitative individuals living in communities of comfort started taking advantage of the situations. They are taking charge of changing the laws. They are causing a huge imbalance.

For example, an imaginary law asking everyone to tolerate vegetarians is bound to create unhappiness in meat lovers. In today's societies, there are gender laws, race laws, food laws etc., which are highly prone to develop despair. Where there are no societies or groups, where each human is free to accept or reject others' choice of happiness or misery, there is no need for any law. There is beauty in such anarchy where humans are totally liberated. It is an unburdened living with total acceptance and surrendering to karma.

OUR UNIQUE EXPERIENCES

We humans are different from each other. Each one of us is a unique entity. Our interaction with the outside world and its impressions inside us are unique. We are unique, alone, engaged in life, and travelling alone. All bonds, friendships and acquaintances are a mere convenience. We act independently although we appear to be a part of the group.

For example, I was severely hurt when I was seven. Can the reader feel my pain? No. The reader may feel empathy. The reader may feel sorry for me, but the reader cannot feel 100% of my hurt experience because my painful experience is unique to me. My sense organs recorded the hurt in a specific space and time and made a memorable impression. However much I wish to forget, it remains a marker until my death. As a conscious entity, I was there beyond that space and time, simultaneously witnessing the experience of and undergoing the hurt. This is unique for each of us. I cannot get a hundred-percent certainty of what each human is be going through. Therefore, though I want to address all the misery migrants are going through, I can only empathise but cannot experience the experiences a hundred percent. Our experiences are unique to us.

Because each and every individual's experiences are so unique, like thumbprints, we can not blanket assume and make laws applicable to a group.

We experience the world using our five sense organs. We taste using our tongues, hear using our ears, feel the touch using our skin, see the world using our eyes, and smell the environment using our noses. Just as our thumbprints are unique, the experience our human consciousness derives from interacting with the world using the five sense organs is unique. It means the enjoyment I derive from eating food is unique to me. The pleasure I derive from listening to music is unique to me. The happiness I get by having sex is unique to me. The enjoyment I derive from smelling a rose with a lovely fragrance is unique to me.

Just as my experiences are unique to me, the experiences which others have are unique to them. Therefore, any law we collectively agree to abide by must consider these unique experiences. Any arbitrarily imposed law that ignores uniqueness causes a miserable experience for the human who does not like the experience the arbitrary law gives them.

ARE WE INTELLIGENT ANIMALS?

We are not capable of greater intelligence than other animals or beings sharing this earth with us. I came across an argument that says humans are great because humans can organise themselves in millions, but I disagree. Red crabs on Christmas Island organise themselves in billions. I do not think humans can gather more than ten million at a single place without trampling ourselves to death in a stampede. Penguins in Antarctica organise themselves in millions without any issue.

So the question is, why do we organise ourselves?! We organise ourselves to know something, survive, or be happy. Even red crabs organise themselves in billions to know where the food is, eat food to survive, and sexually mate to be happy and procreate.

It is just that we humans have excessive pride and arrogance with regard to our own capabilities. We invent things and praise each other for our achievements, while for other animals this does not matter.. For them, we are just another species sharing this earth with them.

OUR GREATEST ADVANTAGE IS OUR UNPREDICTABILITY

Then how did we become to be the apex predators on this earth? How did we land up dominating the world, and how did we start exploiting others? It is because our most significant advantage is our unpredictability. How do a pack of wolves, tigers, or hyenas perceive humans? They may be looking at us as dinner they can't have! Because we are strategically tricky for them to grasp. For example, a hunting lion can predict the speed at which its prey, for example, an antelope runs away. It can plan the hunt. It also knows that an antelope only runs but does not fight back.

But a human, from a lion's perspective, is highly unpredictable. If a human runs using two legs, the hunting lion can predict the running speed, but what if its prey is riding a motorcycle or a car!? It would become impossible for the hunting Lion to predict the speed of a human travelling in a chariot drawn by a number of horses … Also, humans can fight back using many instruments such as knives, spheres, guns, and bombs. They can deploy many methods, such as attack hiding behind an impenetrable sheath made of metal. Or attack from an aeroplane etc., This statistical unpredictability made the lions not bother attacking the humans. The same is the case with the rest of the animals. They do not understand humans because of human unpredictability. Still, some try once in a while, though after failure, they teach their offspring not to attack humans. This is how the evolutionary chain, most animals came to respect humans. This is why they try to move away as much as possible from us when we bother them rather than attack!

Our most significant advantage is our unpredictability. But it has also made us deeply mistrust each other. Exploitative humans use mistrust as a weapon for their exploitation. They enslave the rest of the humans by weaponising mistrust as part of a divide-and-rule policy.

3

TRAITS OF EXPLOITATION, STUPIDITY AND ALTRUISM

"I contend that fortitude in war has its roots in morality; that selection is a search for character, and that war itself is but one more test – the supreme and final test if you will – of character. [...] Character, as Aristotle taught, is a habit, the daily choice of right instead of wrong; it is a moral quality which grows to maturity in peace and is not suddenly developed on the outbreak of war [...] Man's fate in battle is worked out before war begins."[9]

Lord Moran, The Anatomy of Courage

In this chapter, I share the information I learned from elders and from scriptures such as Mahabharata and Ramayana on recognising exploitative and stupid humans so that one can be cautious in one's dealings with them. I also explain how to recognise the traits of altruistic humans so that we can collaborate with them.

Intuitively recognising that you are in the presence of an exploitative individual or a situation requires patience and time to practise. But we can train our minds to instinctively realise that we are in the physical presence of an exploitative individual. Exploitative individuals harbour some or all of the following recognisable traits and external behaviours.

TRAITS OF EXPLOITATIVE HUMANS

1. Excessive pride
2. Arrogance
3. Greedy
4. Lack of empathy
5. Unnecessary use of power
6. Cruelty
7. Warmongering

8. Being violent at both a physical and mental level

9. Making you feel like you are walking on eggshells

10. Having a highly suspicious nature

11. Being prone to rage

12. Withholding information

13. Gaslighting others in your presence

14. Creating gossip and weaponising it

15. Holding grudges for no reason

16. Jealousy

17. Lack of remorse

The above list of traits is not exhaustive. They apply to exploitative individuals, but equally, a group of individuals under an exploitative leader can express the same traits if acting as a single entity, like a gang of medieval raiders involved in slave trading out to catch slaves. For example, a group can act like a single entity and hold a grudge against a single person. So a single individual may know why they are ruining a person's life because their group leader, who is the actual keeper of information, holds a grudge, and the group is blindly executing the exploitative order of the leader. Their survival in the group therefore depends on blind loyalty towards the leader.

The exploitative individuals are highly manipulative. If they need something from you, they will talk sweetly. You will be missing observing the traits mentioned above due to clever concealment. Therefore the best approach is to passively observe how any person behaves when dealing with low-wage earners, people who live on charity or people who are going through unfortunate times in life. Exploitative individuals will not be interested in dealing with people who do not possess any material value for them to exploit, and will treat the meek and hapless with utter disregard.

Since exploitative individuals tend to be very powerful, any slight hesitation from us in following their wishes, commands or orders will invoke rage in them. They can ruin lives in a second. Therefore one has to be highly diligent in dealing with them.

In the previous chapter on human nature, I wrote about human awareness and the triangle of three primal desires. This triangle of three primal desires is hardwired in us. In order to fulfil these three desires, we become social animals, we become teams, and inevitably we get drawn into the company of exploitative individuals. We can use the four quadrants of the human activity diagram to classify the actions of group members. Because humans are prone to shifting from one activity to the other, our Four Quadrants of Human Activity diagram helps us to become aware and conscious of other members.

Even though we are innocent, our desires to know, to survive and be happy take us to places where we think there are opportunities. We become group members. We initially engage with exploitative and stupid individuals because we are unaware of the danger we are walking into. After we recognise the difficult situation we have got into, we try to disengage. But the laws and social customs we built around us make it difficult to disentangle without a complaint or a courtroom battle.

In addition, the fear factor kicks in to prevent us from disengaging. The fear that we may lose everything we hard-earned makes us hesitate.

For example, the world-famous musician Tina Turner, who died recently, was an outstanding singer, who won many Grammys, but was married to Ike Turner, who married her only for her money.

Later he became so abusive that she had to endure severe beatings from him. He was the exploitative individual in their relationship. He was highly abusive. Initially what started as a great love between two highly talented individuals became an abusive and exploitative relationship. There was no love remained in that supposed to be a husband and wife relationship. Finally, she decided to leave him. But she became penniless after she left because he wrote all her contracts in his name, and she innocently listened to everything he said. She was literally left penniless after their divorce in spite of all the money she earned. This is what I call an exploitative relationship. She had to rebuild her life. But she was naturally talented; and so was able to rebuild her life quite successfully. We are all born with some kind of talent, there are many talents out there but skill is what we develop further using our talent. Exploitative individuals get attracted to talent. Many talented individuals get trapped by exploitative individuals. It requires skill to not get trapped that is why it gets very difficult for them to disengage. Unfortunately not all talented people are blessed with skills.

Exploitative individuals do not take disengagement kindly. They tend to bear grudges and plot against their victims for a lifetime. In fulfilling their grudge, they exploit everyone who trusts them and is in their inner circle as team members. Eventually, everyone who works for and works against the exploitative individual gets ruined. There is only one winner in the game any exploitative individual plays – themselves.

From the Four Quadrants of Human Activity diagram, we saw that the nature of an exploitative individual is to gain for themselves while ruining others. They act with an entitled mentality destroying us and involving everyone in their circle to destroy us, –eventually destroying those who help them as well. They act as if it is their birthright to ruin everyone around them!

We can compare innocent engagement with an exploitative individual and our eventual wish to disengage to driving on a motorway at high speed. Imagine driving on a highway and realising you took a wrong turn. As a result, you are now going in the wrong direction. Entanglement, such as a business engagement with an exploitative individual, is like recognising that you took a wrong turn on a motorway. We know that transactions with exploitative humans will eventually ruin us. So why continue such engagement unless we are stupid or altruistic? As ordinary humans, our instinct tells us to disengage.

But what can our immediate reaction be? Can we slam on our brakes in the middle of the highway? No, because that will put our lives and the lives of other innocent drivers in danger. Similarly, sudden disengagement from an exploitative individual could result in unwanted consequences. Consequently, we must have a proper exit strategy.

Also, one has to be mindful of the fact that exploitative individuals may have already created a trap, as a result of which finding an exit would be extremely difficult! Destroying others is of no consequence to exploitative individuals, so they use everything in their power to keep their victims trapped till they have sucked the life out of them.

As I explained using the Four Quadrants of Human Activity diagram, any of us can get tempted to participate in an exploitative action. Human actions are sometimes exploitative, while sometimes they may be altruistic, ordinary or stupid. We can watch out for exploitative actions. But disengaging requires considerable dispassion.

The best course of action to stop exploitation is non-violent disengagement. victims of exploitative individuals must disengage from the emotions of anger and revenge.

Patience, perseverance and waiting for the right opportunity to exit are excellent strategies to disengage from exploitation. Moderately regular practice of meditation techniques, such as recognising the light between the eyebrows while meditating and dispassion towards the excessive desire which brought us into the presence of the exploitative individual, will help us stay clear of the danger.

Then what about the people who become exploitative? There are three powerful emotions which propel us into acting in an exploitative manner. Therefore, those who do not wish to be exploitative must be extremely careful. They must be mindful of the three compelling emotions – excessive desire, cognitive dissonance and greed. Stay away from satiating any one of these three. These emotions are insatiable. They act like a dark and powerful vortex where light does not shine. Exploitative individuals often are in the spell of these three emotions. As a consequence, they destroy the world in their ignorance. The best world for the species is the world where each human does self-introspection and regulates the rise of these three emotions.

I advise seeking the light between the eyebrows meditation technique because the light represents our awareness. Meditation to see the light in us helps us recognise our efforts to succeed as ordinary humans. Seeking light meditation helps us introspect. Meditation helps us to see if we are becoming exploitative humans by falling prey to the three powerful destructive emotions, Desire, Cognitive dissonance and Greed. Meditation helps us reflect upon our human stupidity in day-to-day actions.

INSTRUMENTS OF EXPLOITATION

We call the exploiters who act alone fraudsters, extortionists, blackmailers, hustlers, scammers or embezzlers; they are nearly everywhere. We find a certain number of exploitative humans in every human-powered system. Some exploitative humans act alone, some start businesses and others embed themselves in large corporations or join governments. It does not matter which type of government it is – monarchies, dictatorships, nation-states, democracies or plutocracies; we will find humans with exploitative tendencies embedded everywhere. Corruption is the instrument of exploitation for the people embedded in government structures. They keep playing the power game, which I explained about in the next chapter.

The trail of human misery caused by exploiters depends on the level of the chain of command in which they position themselves in the system. Every human seeks peace, tranquillity, the dignity of labour and the correct value they deserve for their work. However, exploitative humans in the structure deny these and cause misery. Many businesses fail not because there is a lack of vision in the leadership but because they may not be aware of or become too complacent with an exploitative human embedded in the structure of their system.

EXPLOITATION AND FRAUDS

Individuals with an exploitative nature commit fraud. Through these frauds, they gain riches for themselves while ruining others. Not all acts of exploitation are considered a crime in the eyes of the law. But we can recognise the underlying acts of exploitation by looking at the greedy excesses of amounts gained by individuals, corporations and governments manned by exploitative individuals.

Exploitative forces of power hide the trail of their exploitative acts by creating artificial countries where laws help them hide their wealth. Therefore, all the individual country laws that helped exploitative individuals hide their greed will become extinct when we evolve as humans without borders. Removing restrictions imposed by countries helps the global flow of wealth. It also helps us reset the actual derivative value of each object, each commodity and each resource we humans desire and deserve for our survival as a species.

The problem of exploitative forces in power is not faced just by a single country. In almost all countries, these forces have infested like termites, eating away human empathy's generous spirit. The victims of these exploitative forces undergo economic poverty. Deprived of their natural state of happiness, survival and knowledge, they suffer trauma and psychological problems. And eventually, to escape systematic exploitation, some of these victims immigrate. They cross borders seeking a better world. But unfortunately, exploitation is everywhere in all countries. Because humans participate in exploitative actions, there is no escape; therefore, instead of running away from the problem, every human victim must take a resolute non-violent stand against tyranny, oppression and ruthless exploitation. The change one expects in this world must begin with the individual seeking the change. There is a force called soul force. It has excellent power. We can invoke this power that can bring change even in the cruellest of humans.

Every exploiting individual must realise one thing. The day of reckoning will come. They cannot escape the karma of their cruel deeds. Mother Earth nourished them. Out of the dust they came, and into dust they go. Every human is answerable to the earth upon which they live. Exploitative humans are no exception. Every human can use the Four Quadrants of Human Activity diagram to self-introspect their actions.

THE STORY OF A FOX AND EARTH

To illustrate the point that there is no escape even for the exploiters, let me narrate a story. Once upon a time, a very cunning fox lived on borrowing money and enjoying life. The crafty Fox only knew how to borrow money but never used to repay it. Therefore, after getting victimised by Fox's cunning borrowing tactics, the whole neighbourhood realised that Fox never pays back the money, so nobody was ready to lend. The fox desperately wanted to find someone who it could exploit. But it found no one.

Then all of a sudden, the fox noticed Mother Earth. Mother Earth is very loving, ever-smiling, always forgiving and full of patience. So the fox decided to con Mother Earth. So crafty Fox thought of deceiving the innocent Earth!

The fox approached Mother Earth and begged her to loan him a dollar. Mother Earth, always helpful, agreed to lend a dollar to the fox but on one condition, that Fox must pay back the dollar in seven days. The cunning Fox was thrilled with the condition because it never intended to pay back anyway.

So the Earth loaned a dollar to the fox. The fox enjoyed spending the dollar. Seven days passed, and the time had come for the fox to pay back the loan. Fox knew it had to pay back the loan. Therefore it decided to deploy its old tactics. It wanted to escape from Earth. So in order to escape from Earth, the fox started running away. After running for a few hours, fox thought Mother Earth would not be able to come there and ask for her money. So it decided to take a rest. But Mother Earth appeared there and asked, 'Oh Fox, I loaned you a dollar on condition that you pay back in seven days. It is time to pay me back.'

The cunning fox was surprised. It did not understand how Mother Earth had caught him up. So the fox started running away again. It ran for another few hours. But Mother Earth appeared there too, asking the fox to pay back. The fox ran again. Thus, the fox ran for so long to escape Earth that it died of exhaustion in the end. The fox never realised that it was running *on* Mother Earth but not *away* from it. The mother earth in this story is called Karma. There is no escape from Karma! We pay for all our deeds when Karma catches us up.

The moral of the story is that nobody can escape the consequences of exploitation. Nature is everywhere. Everyone on earth dies in one of those seven days, Sunday, Monday, Tuesday, Wednesday, Thursday, Friday and Saturday. We never hear the story of any person who died some other day other than these seven days. Every exploitation is answerable to Earth. It keeps reminding us of the exploitation we are doing through global storms, floods, landslides and many other violent climate-related events. Instead of trying to escape, one has to self-introspect, acknowledge their inner nature and do something about it.

SOME OF THE FRAUDS AND THEIR IMPACT

We can get a list of many frauds worldwide if we use any internet search engine. We can find many corrupt and nepotist politicians, dictators and other individuals who exploit society.. Search for Theranos fraud, OneCoin fraud. An estimated three million people lost their money to this fraud. Also, search for Africans who have been scammed by their dictators. Search for corrupt politicians. The worldwide negative impact caused by each exploitative individual is immeasurable.

Let us look at some of the frauds which have caused great misery. Frauds happen around the world all the time. Not all scams come to light. But I narrate below a few of the well-known and well-documented frauds. Frauds are caused by exploitative individuals who fail to see the human misery their actions would cause.

WORLDCOM FRAUD

WorldCom fraud was an estimated US $30 billion. As a result, 17,000 employees lost their jobs. A NewYork-based pension fund lost $300 million.

ENRON FRAUD

Enron Corporation was one of the largest U.S. energy commodities. It was ranked seventh among America's largest and most profitable companies in 2000. In December 2001, it filed for bankruptcy. Thousands of employees lost their jobs. According to investigations, Enron was disguising losses and concealing its debts. Enron's shareholders lost an estimated $74 billion in the four years before the company's bankruptcy, and $40 to $45 billion was attributed to fraud. Only a handful of top executives got convicted and spent jail terms. This fraud also resulted in one of the accounting giants, Arthur Andersen, collapsing. Overall, it has been estimated that approximately 85,000 people, directly or indirectly connected to these large firms, lost their jobs, their savings dwindled, and shareholders' money evaporated. All resulted from a few top bosses who failed to see the consequences of their exploitative actions. All of their actions fall into either the Exploitative or Stupid quadrants of the human activity diagram.

FTX CRYPTO EXCHANGE FRAUD

This is an interesting fraud to look at. FTX is a company that operated a cryptocurrency exchange and crypto hedge fund. It had over one million users. It was one of the top five cryptocurrency exchanges by volume. Its co-founder, Sam Bankman-Fried, appeared to be an altruistic individual, and he claimed he had no interest in personal gain (thus positioning himself in the Altruistic Human quadrant in the Four Modes of Human Activity diagram).

Sam Bankman-Fried clicked all the right buttons through his actions. He cooperated with authorities, whereas the other crypto traders were reluctant to engage with federal authorities. He slept on a couch. He spoke like a sage. He said that he was going to donate away all his wealth etc. All his actions brought him popularity. It evoked sympathy in the forces of power in people who fall into the quadrant of ordinary humans.. Even world-famous politicians such as ex-British Prime Minister Tony Blair and ex-US president Bill Clinton attended conferences organised by FTX and appeared on the same stage with Sam Bankman-Fried. We must wonder what motivated Tony Blair or Bill Clinton to endorse FTX. We also don't know why or what motivated many world-class celebrities to advocate FTX. Was it money, altruism, exploitation or simple human stupidity? Where will all these celebrities place their actions with FTX when they get a chance to tick a box in the Four Quadrants of Human Activity diagram? They alone will know the answer to why they did what they did.

We humans tend to fall for any actions of altruism because our conscience goads us, inspiring us to be altruistic. There is an element of altruism hardwired in all of us. It is hardwired in our DNA that the world can not survive without those who can not sacrifice themselves. The world requires sacrifices.

We all intrinsically know that there is an element of altruism in us. Still, we will never know when this altruism will kick in! For example, we all know the story of Oskar Schindler, who saved many Jews from execution. The famous multi-award-winning movie *Schindler's List*, directed by Steven Spielberg, is made from Oskar Schindler's story.

Oskar Schindler was a German industrialist and member of the Nazi party. He saved many of his Jewish employees after witnessing the persecution of Jews in Poland. He was a German who wanted to exploit cheap labour in concentration camps. But eventually, he turned out to be an altruist. He decided to spend all his money to buy freedom for the Jews. This is an example that there is always a chance for redemption for everyone, including exploitative individuals! We, humans, can instinctively recognise altruism in other people. This is the reason we give out expressions of praise like 'He's a good person', 'she's a good person', 'he's an angel,' etc.

Sam Bankman-Fried he considered himself an altruist, but his actions at the helm while running the FTX business had attracted many exploitative individuals. This is the reason why in excess of an estimated US $10 billion was lost to fraud. The impact FTX fraud caused on ordinary, rule-abiding traders from around the world is colossal. Many pension funds invested in FTX lost their money.

Sam Bankman-Fried was arrested, and the collapse of FTX is still being investigated while writing this book. But it is interesting to plot his actions and the actions of other participants in FTX on the Four Quadrants of Human Activity diagram. Sam Bankman-Fried started his journey in the top right-hand area as an ordinary human Then he appeared to be an altruist through his statements, such as announcing that he would donate away all his wealth. Later he became a part of the exploitative individuals area by allowing an incestuous business relationship between FTX and Alameda Research, the businesses he co-founded. And finally, after getting arrested, he descended to the bottom-left quadrant by ruining himself and others with his actions, proving himself to be stupid.

TRAITS OF STUPID HUMANS

Almost all stupid individuals emerge from exploitative individuals. The exploitative individuals realise that they have been stupid right from the beginning when the exploitative action they engaged in backfires. However, the following are the few points which we find extra in stupid humans in addition to the traits already mentioned.

1. Profound ignorance
2. No boundaries
3. Excessive unregulated desires
4. Unjustified jealousy
5. Acting with a sense of entitlement
6. No consideration of an alternative viewpoint
7. Indiscriminate use of power
8. Indiscriminate in actions
9. Ruining others
10. Ruining themselves

Unfortunately, we can not expect any remorse or course correction from stupid individuals. They descend into a mad rage and destroy themselves and their victims. For example, all shooters participating in mass shooting activities are stupid humans. They get killed or jailed for life for their actions, but they ruin many lives in their final act of stupidity.

THE NATURE OF ALTRUISM

Altruism is a fascinating phenomenon. It involves sacrifice. Any person who sacrifices happiness, safety and knowledge for the greater good of humanity can be called an altruistic human. But the question is: why sacrifice when our experience informs us that the world is thankless, highly selfish and brutal? People will take advantage of altruistic people. It is the altruistic people who suffer the most. So, why do it? Why do such a thankless job of helping people out of their misery? Why do altruistic humans strive to provide happiness for free, protect people from danger, and give away vital knowledge to help people thrive?!

An ancient Indian scripture called *Rigveda* gives a fascinating insight into altruism. *Rigveda* is a compilation of received revelations by people of wisdom called seers. Western histories estimate it to have been compiled between 1500 and 1000 BCE, whereas Indian traditional Vedic scholars who are born and brought up in India and study vedas from traditional sclools, believe *Rigveda* to be tens of thousands of years old. *Rigveda* contains a hymn called *Purusha Suktam*, the 90th hymn of the 10th Mandala of the *Rigveda*. The hymn is a description of the creation of the universe and the nature of the Supreme Being or 'Virat Purusha'. The logic explaining the Supreme Being says that only ONE being exists. He alone is in this universe. You, the reader, and I, the writer, are not there, but we are ONE. It asks us to realise and arrive at this cosmic truth – that you and I are not separate but one – through logic.

In the preamble of this book, I narrated a story that at the beginning of time, this earth was inhabited by only two people, a man and a woman. How they came to be is explained in *Purusha Suktam*. Purusha, an androgynous primal human, upon his own will, through primordial self-sacrifice, divided himself into man and woman. And that is how the world we know came to be.

We all eat food. Our food comes from the earth. An apple that you eat comes from the earth. An apple that I eat also comes from the earth. We digest the apple, which nourishes us and becomes a part of our physical body. Though the apple may be the same, after we consume it gives us distinctive identities. The apple which Tom ate gets digested but Tom remains as Tom only. The apple Harry ate makes him remain as Harry only. The earth is the same, and the apple that came out of it is the same, but why even after eating the apple of same taste, smell and place or origin does not make Tom and Harry similar? Instead, Tom remains Tom and Harry remains Harry? This is the mystery of creation. Humans consume the same earth, drink the same water, breathe the same air, and act distinctively. We should not be different, but we are different! The logic of the Supreme Being in Rigveda says there is only one being. It is an error to think that there are many. The whole world is nothing but that being. It is everything and everywhere.

Therefore, at a very core level, we all humans are nothing but part and parcel of that supreme being, like individual cells in the same body! There are now some eight and a half billion human beings and trillions of other beings; all are just ONE. Following the logic where though we are consuming same resources we are acting distinctive, gives us an insight that we are ONE. But our ego says we are different. This concept is difficult to grasp, but we can feel it! A person who very strongly feels that he is not separate from this universe and acts for the welfare of the whole world is an altruist. The fact remains we are just ONE, and the creation is a homogeneous mass of consciousness. Therefore, altruism can be logically explained as an act of that ONE being protecting itself.

Army ant soldiers sacrifice themselves in a fight because at a very core level they do not feel separate. In killing themselves, by sacrificing themselves for the sake of the colony, they are living. They never even seem to feel that they are dying. They are not separate from the rest of the ants. Though we see billions of different ants in the same colony, they are symbiotic.

Therefore, an altruistic human is someone who is genetically hardwired to help, to sacrifice personal comfort, safety and security for the sake of others.

TRAITS OF ALTRUISTIC HUMANS

The following are the traits we can witness in Altruist humans.

1. No hatred towards any being
2. Absence of cognitive dissonance
3. Friendliness
4. Compassion
5. Freedom from attachment
6. Freedom from egoism
7. Maintains a balanced mind between pleasure and pain
8. Forgiving nature
9. Contented nature
10. Shows steadiness in meditation
11. Is self-controlled
12. Tranquillity of mind
13. Has firm conviction in their mission

14. Surrenders the mind and intellect to the supreme

15. Charity in mind

16. Puts others before themselves

17. Is peaceful

18. Is fearless

19. Never second guesses their actions

4

THE NATURE OF EXPLOITATIVE POWER

Exploitation requires power. There are two ways of achieving anything from others. One is the way of love, and the other is the way of power.

Love is a natural way. Love needs no manipulation. Love has no scope for exploitation. It is more an unconditional yearning to give than any eagerness to take. Love has no boundaries. It forgives quickly and offers peace to the person who cultivates it in their heart. Love is ever forgiving. In love, there is no scope for deception. Love is like a river of nectarine. Its sweet flow can heal broken hearts and mend invisible mental wounds. Love is the gift God gave to humankind. To love is the greatest gift one can offer, but to be loved is a rare privilege. This is why not everyone can feel love. Many who are deprived of love go on to develop exploitative and stupid personalities. Love is not lust. In lust, physical bodies desire to merge.

In comparison, love is merging one's psychological personality with the universal. The journey of love starts with loving one's family, children and neighbours, but as the capacity to love grows, so grows the vision to spread love universally. Love is a scarce commodity.

Power leads to exploitation. One needs power in the absence of love. Power is ruthless, and exploitation backed by power is highly manipulative. Only those who are deprived of love are capable of exploitation. Psychopaths, sociopaths and narcissists do not know what love is. Therefore, they crave power because power makes them achieve what others achieve through love. But power deprived of love does not last long. Consequently, one must start cultivating love.

Power is to be able to do better. Power is to know better, to feel better, happy and to be able to survive better. In primitive societies, a person who can hunt better using intelligence is considered powerful. Whoever can gather better is powerful.

Power is to control whatever others value. All humans love happiness, survival and knowledge. Therefore whoever can provide these to those who follow them is the most powerful. Those who are in love unconditionally yearn to provide these three to others. They want to see their loved ones be happy, survive, and be knowledgeable. On the contrary, in power games, those who are significantly powerful also hold the capability to deny these three to others; this is why power-play involves both provision and denial.

In the olden days, in family units, fathers used to go out to hunt, use weapons to defend the family, etc. Mothers used to offer their children love, nourishment and protection while their father was away bringing them food. Both father and mother provided happiness to children through their love, survival through their protection and the knowledge they gained of how to be happy and survive.

Happiness, survival and knowledge are necessary for all humans. Especially there must be mentors who can help children grow confidently in societies. In large family units, many men and women share responsibilities. They all strive to provide happiness, survival and knowledge to their family. But whoever excels in delivering the best enjoyment, survival, and knowledge becomes powerful within the family. The rest of the family unit submits to that most powerful member of the family.

As civilisation grew, macro-families became micro and fatherless or motherless single families. Modern-day humans changed how we live. Children are deprived of watching the power-play because of the absence of many adults who can participate in the social game of providing happiness, survival and knowledge. No wonder modern-day humans are hooked on watching reality shows because they see the drama of happiness, survival and knowledge in these reality shows!

But how about disagreements in the family? They get sorted due to love. Because there is love, there is forgiveness and understanding. The blood bond is the thickest. We are still hardwired to love our siblings and other family members, however much they hurt us! It is an invisible but strong bond.

Children who grow up without a loving family or in the absence of many family members tend to become confused. In the absence of family or in addition to what a family offers, most modern-day governments provide happiness, survival and knowledge to their citizens. Governments rely on employed humans to provide these. Governments set out rules and regulations on how to provide happiness, survival and knowledge.

But why would any employee employed by the government necessarily care about what happens to abandoned children, even if many workers in social care do? These employees responsible for the children's welfare are a part of the system. Unfortunately, some of these humans though they routinely follow the rules and regulations, fail to see the larger picture. They follow the rules but lack the essential love a large family unit can provide. Rules and regulations require enforcement. Enforcement means power. Power in the absence of love is prone to corruption. The greater the power, the greater the corruption. This corrupt mentality leads to exploitation. Governments must encourage large family units to live together. But such families should not depend on the state handouts for their happiness, survival and knowledge!

EXPLOITATIVE POWER

Exploitation is to deprive others of what they deserve. All humans deserve to be happy, to survive and to know. Exploitation is to deny others any of these three but to gain it for oneself. Remember our Four Quadrants of Human Activity diagram. Exploitative humans help themselves while ruining others! To ruin others means making others feel miserable by denying happiness, intimidating others with threats and violence, and keeping secrets to deprive others of proper knowledge.

For example, we seek sex for pleasure. To restrict any human to a single sexual partner is to exercise control, thus taking power over us. Out of our sexual activity children are born. We develop a deep bond with our offspring, which we call family. Whoever controls how many children we can have has power over us. By denying the urge to seek sexual partners, they hold power over us. Similarly, we read books for happiness and watch drama and TV for pleasure. But whoever controls what kind of books we can read and what type of dramas and TV shows we can watch have power over us. If we have personal purchasing power, then we are happy. We can buy what we think is giving us happiness. By excluding us from economic activity, exploitative humans hold power over us. All of us want to feel safe. We want to survive. Whoever provides us with that safety has power over us.

Power is not an issue as long as the person yielding that power uses it with the utmost discretion. The powerful person must act as a sacred trustee, not a violent tyrant! Power is fluid. It does not stay for long at any single place for a long time.

History proves that every human generation witnesses the rise of a few hundred powerful leaders. It is these individuals with power ultimately decide the laws that govern, the direction that their country must take, the wars they must fight etc., The rest of the people are obedient followers of the orders of these powerful people. No person who holds power is immortal! We do not even have any monuments to some of the most powerful people in history. Even their burial sites are not available. They became a speck of insignificant dust for nature, and we only talk about them as history.

Every generation hands over control of their lives to the hands of chosen leaders. The next generation pushes aside the ageing leader. Most probably, the generation after that witnesses the burial of that leader. Thus the life of a leader is going up an escalator with a finite number of steps. Each step is the year they rule. After going up the escalator, they will have to get down. Otherwise, the mechanical motion inside the escalator ruthlessly pushes them to get off. Also, someone else who is standing in line to be the next leader will push them aside.

We humans are organic beings. We age. We suffer from sickness. We are accident-prone. Every one of us perishes in time, without exception. Therefore time is the most powerful thing because it controls even the most powerful leaders. In time, leaders rise and fall. This is why the person with power must recognise the greatness of time and be humble. With all humility, they must act as a trustee to the people who will follow them. They must be aware of generational changes and must graciously give up the leadership to the leader chosen by the next generation.

EXPLOITATIVE LEADERS

Exploitative leaders are the people who fall into the top left-hand quadrant of diagram. They become leaders to help themselves and ruin the subjects they rule. Many dictators from around the world fall into this category.

A leader is also a human like any other. They go through the same human emotions in their day-to-day life. They may also perform akratic activities. But some leaders, drunk by the power they enjoy, become blind to the time. They get into the delusion that their position is permanent and that they are somehow immortal! In such a delusion, they get caught up in the net of three powerful emotions: Excessive Desire, Cognitive dissonance and Greed.

I explained earlier how family plays a role in shaping a child into adulthood. Exploitative leaders tend to lack a strong family bond. They come from a highly dysfunctional family. A family which does not hold its members in love but binds them through a myriad of rules is a dysfunctional family.

Some exploitative leaders are psychopaths, mentally unwell people who cleverly disguise their chaotic inner personalities to stay in power. Leaders who emerge out of dysfunctional families become nepotistic, creating quasi-dynasties. They keep control and power within their family, passing it to their offspring. That means the original exploitative leader continues living through his offspring's actions. They do not just become nepotistic, but they also became corrupt. In their greed, they use every opportunity available to accumulate wealth which can last for generations.

Exploitative leaders create exploitative forces. They create and give rise to exploitative power. Some countries get caught in the grip of these leaders for generations. Leaders get selected within the family. People who oppose such exploitative families get brutally crushed. Thus giving rise to the refugee crisis. But history has proven that none of these dynasties continues forever. The time will come when the exploitative leaders, their power circles and the exploitative forces will collapse and become dust.

Time tells the victims of exploitation not to give up hope. Generations may suffer under tyranny, but time is a great answer. Time is the greatest healer. And in time, everything happens. Humans are not robots, but organic beings. We go through organic stages of life. These stages include birth, childhood, youth, adulthood, ageing and death. Every exploitative human also goes through these stages. They will get ruthlessly pushed aside by time during the stages of ageing and death. Therefore victims should not lose hope. They must wait for time and the right opportunity.

POWER IS A GAME FOR EXPLOITATIVE LEADERS

Power is a skill. It requires a certain amount of deception to be used by those who choose to play it. There are two types of power: natural power and augmented power.

Natural power is like that of an athlete who wins a race because they are naturally powerful. But what if some, in their blind desire to succeed, augment it using performance-enhancing drugs? Such power is called augmented power. Exploitative Leaders and exploitative countries expand their power through augmented means, using police, military and clandestine services. But because power is fluid, time-bound and highly influenced by various external factors such as time, the leaders who depend heavily on augmented power become highly paranoid. History informs us that dictators such as Hitler, Mussolini, and many other dictators worldwide became paranoid. They died a miserable and lonely death because they suspected even their augmented power! For example, Stalin did not go to a hospital in his own city because he did not trust the doctors! He believed they were more interested in killing him than helping him.

WHEN IS POWER AN OBSTACLE

Power becomes an obstacle when the people who hold power are under the influence or trapped by the exploitative forces entrenched in the governance circles. It becomes a problem when anyone tries to take power by controlling experiences unique to each person. To feel happy is an experience, to survive better is an experience, and to gain knowledge is an experience. These are unique to each person. The world has become problematic because, as far as human history goes, humans are increasingly trying to manage experiences unique to each person as a group rather than individually. Individuals may become a part of a group, but their experiences are not group experiences. As a result, there are always disagreements within a group. Power becomes an obstacle for the leaders who use augmented power to control such groups.

A quote attributed to Einstein says that it is stupid to do the same experiment again and again but expect different results[11]. We have experimented enough with groups formed by individuals with unique experiences. It is time to disband the groups and give each human the true power they rightly deserve!

UNDERMINING DEMOCRACY

People who gather together with the sole intention of exploiting become an exploitative force of power. These exploitative forces of power sit very comfortably inside the countries that value democracy.

Indeed, these forces enjoy all the levers provided by the system of democracy. Still, due to their nature of exploitation, they undermine democracy. In other forms of governance, such as monarchies and dictatorships, it would be difficult to pinpoint the force which is causing the exploitation because of a lack of transparency. But democracies do not suffer from a lack of transparency, which is why we clearly see when things do not work how they are supposed to. Therefore, when things go wrong when things do not work as we expected, we can assume that there are forces of exploitation at work.

For example, the police forces are supposed to uphold the constitutional rights of all citizens. Civil servants are supposed to serve all citizens without any discrimination. But when we see a group of police fail to protect a hapless citizen, or a group of civil servants harassing a citizen, delaying or derailing what that person truly deserves, we know there are exploitative forces behind the scenes.

Like termites, these forces are self-serving and greedy; they are exploitative in nature, with no care for what impact their senseless actions will have on the ordinary god-fearing citizens of democratic countries who are amicably living their daily life. But eventually, these exploitative individuals get caught, and a course correction gets initiated by the altruistic politicians who yield power but not for their personal gain.

Reactive course correction occurs when people's power is present in republics and democracies. But misery is still present in such countries for some citizens who are reluctant to exercise their civil rights because they are, perhaps, afraid of consequences from exploitative individuals in power.

WE WAR BECAUSE WE FEAR

Then what about the military as a force? Are they exploitative? Soldiers fighting in a battle for their country belong to both the exploitative human quadrant and also to the altruist human quadrant. Which quadrant their action falls under needs to be clarified, and it depends on which side we stand on and look at the situation.

Soldiers of exploitation: The soldier in one quadrant is helping himself by ruining others. He kills others who are enemies. You may wonder, how is he helping himself? He is helping himself by following orders. If he says no to specific orders, he gets court-martialed. Therefore, fearing for their life, soldiers follow orders. They kill whoever their high command orders them to kill. This is one of the reasons why, in war crimes investigations, the people with high authority who are in charge of the perpetrators' actions are hauled in front of justice, and rightly so.

Soldiers of altruism: During the Second World War, many altruistic German soldiers and officers refused to follow the orders of the tyrannical dictator Hitler. As a consequence, they were all shot to death. When a soldier dies in battle, they sacrifice themselves, and in their death, they helped their fellow citizens. Therefore such a human is an altruistic human.

Every war is an act of exploitation. Is it possible for us to avoid wars? Yes, we can prevent wars when we stop excessively fearing, start using peace to settle our differences and stop exploiting others for our selfish means. We can avert wars when the globe acts as one family. In a family, there is love. Families are made of a profound human bond. Family members tend to forgive quickly. There will be disagreements, but a family puts maximum effort into avoiding conflicts.

As hunter-gatherers, we were family units. All family members provided happiness, security and knowledge to the children. These family units became tribes based on the same three desires – happiness, survival, and knowledge. A person who could best provide these three to all the members of the tribe became the leader of the tribe. These tribes became the subjects of a king and his kingdom. A king who could best provide the best of happiness, survival and knowledge was appreciated and the king who did not provide these was revolted against. As civilisations grew, tribal villages turned into regions for administrative purposes.

What is administration? It is to give the maximum happiness, survivability and knowledge to the maximum number of people. Any administration that failed to provide these three things adequately was considered a failure. These administrative regions grouped together became countries. Countries drew borders and employed military, police and clandestine services to help them in administration. But as we grew, our exploitative governance structures slowly destroyed our family values, resulting in monumental societal calamities. In our eagerness to grow, we gave up traditional family values that had been good for us and helped us survive.

Every human, no matter which tribe they belong to, which village they dwell in or which country they are a citizen of, deserves to be happy, to survive and to have the right to information. Any human who does not get these three wishes fulfilled considers the tribe they belong to as a failed tribe, the village they belong to as a failed village, the administration that is supposed to help them as a failed administration, and the country they belong to as a failed country. Humans who consider that they are let down will not sit quietly. They will try to change their status quo; thus, many become refugees. Some suffer silently without making any noise. There are various other factors which result in citizens suffering without complaining. These hapless individuals remain silent and walk to their graves. We never get to hear their stories.

Humans do suffer globally. Every human experience is a unique experience. Though international administrations consider some countries safe, some humans suffer in these countries too. Therefore, migration happens from these countries as well. But because they are considered safe countries, the silently suffering citizens can not become refugees or claim refugee status in other safe countries. In the rest of the countries, autocracies and dictatorships create enormous problems for their citizens.

Why are homeless people living in abject poverty, suffering from inadequate healthcare, etc.? We never get to hear the individual stories because humanity is nowadays not facilitating altruistic individuals from coming to power and staying in power.

Everyone is a loser in the hands of exploiters. Exploiting forces use the laws and policies which are created by their countries to exploit the resources of other countries. Still, they did not proportionately share the riches with their country. For example, the forces that worked for colonial powers did not share the wealth with their fellow countrymen. Though taxes get paid, they are not enough.

Power in the hands of exploitative individuals is dangerous. We never know why Abraham Lincoln was assassinated. Why was President JFK assassinated? Why so many aspiring leaders in Africa were assassinated? In India, Prime Minister Indira Gandhi and, after a few years, her son, who was also Prime Minister, were assassinated. In Pakistan, President Benazir Bhutto was assassinated. There are scores of tales of assassinations and orchestrated political downfalling. Still, we will never know the real reasons behind these happenings. But we only know that there are exploitative forces behind the scenes behind all these assassinations.

We want to sort out the problems of the world. We created countries. We have created laws and applied them in those countries. But problems persisted. If we want Love, Peace and Prosperity for the maximum number of people, then we must change how we solve problems. We must use a different equation. A new social architecture.

5

THE DESTRUCTIVE STATE OF COGNITIVE DISSONANCE

"We do not see things as they are. We see them as we are." [12]

The Talmud

THE NATURE OF COGNITIVE DISSONANCE

The restlessness any individual feels when recognising difference is called cognitive dissonance. Cognitive dissonance drives the world mad, contributing to the global refugee crisis. Therefore it is essential to understand its nature and impact, as described in this chapter. The Hindu holy book *Bhagavad Gita* explains cognitive dissonance as a destructive state of mind.

The modern-day definition of cognitive dissonance is given by Leon Festinger, who defined it as:

"A state of mental discomfort that arises from holding two different beliefs or values" [13]

Leon Festinger, Theory of cognitive dissonance, 1975

An orthodox religious believer liked religious leaders who preached the views he held dearly. He adored those leaders and would do anything that the leader said without question. One day he came across a non-believer who started arguing about the futility of religious belief. The non-believer opponent called the religious leaders idiots. This enraged the believer, and in a fit of rage, he picked up a shotgun and killed the nonbeliever. That fit of rage is the effect of cognitive dissonance!

Any person who picks up arms and chooses to settle verbal arguments using physical or clandestine violence is undergoing the mental ill health of cognitive dissonance.

Some people naturally self-regulate and do not undergo the ill effects of cognitive dissonance. But others don't! And these individuals are dangerous. They are a danger to themselves and to fellow humanity while under the mad, destructive spell of cognitive dissonance.

Let us reimagine a new world without order as we knew it. I am not in favour of any new world order. Because humans have to be free, let each human be the master of their own destiny. We humans are unique. Our thumbprints are unique, our retina prints are unique, and the way thoughts arise in our minds is unique. We are so unique, yet we get restless when we find individuals acting differently, thinking differently, eating different food or praying to a different god!

The individuals in power who undergo cognitive dissonance concern me the most. This is why I do not prefer a new world order of government. What if the agreed order of things is not followed, and the individual who is enforcing the order is undergoing cognitive dissonance?! It would be a great disaster. I can give many modern-day examples of such disasters but let me give you an example from colonial India.

During the British Raj in India, a General called Sir Michael O'Dwyer ordered that there be no public congregations of large numbers of people. But because there was a festival, people did gather in a park called Jallianwala Bagh. Sir Michael O'Dwyer underwent cognitive dissonance and asked his men to open fire. Thousands of women, men and children who were celebrating were massacred. It was a great human disaster[14].

Sir Michael O'Dwyer did not recognise that even though he gave an order, people are so unique that they may not have understood it.

Some may have never heard of it. And some may have deliberately ignored it. So why be so crazily violent towards people not following orders?! This was because General Sir Michael O'Dwyer did not have the mental capacity to be understanding and compassionate. But such Sir Michael O'Dwyers get extremely dangerous when they have power.

People like Sir Michael O'Dwyers of colonial India exist even today in modern governments across all countries. They may not be so openly violent, but they do have the power to ruin the lives of citizens.

Here are some more examples of the destructive power of cognitive dissonance.

1. The killing of Black American George Floyd by the US police officer who sat on his neck.. (Hill, 2020)[15]
2. The attack on Charlie Hebdo cartoonists.. (Petrikowski, 2019)[16]
3. Attacks on people in homosexual relationships.
4. Attacks on people who are in a polygamous relationship.
5. Militant attacks in the name of some activism.

WEAPONISATION OF COGNITIVE DISSONANCE

Some exploitative humans are experts at weaponising cognitive dissonance. For example, Fascist dictator Hitler blamed Jews for all the Germans' troubles before World War II. His supporters peddled fake news against Jews. Germans got angry with Jews and gave absolute power to Hitler, who went on to implement his evil plans against Jews by exterminating them, calling it the Final Solution. Thus, Hitler weaponised cognitive dissonance, cultivated it in his citizens using fake propaganda, and exterminated millions of Jews.

Military generals create coups to grab power by weaponising cognitive dissonance. Another example is Idi Amin of Uganda. Let us analyse his actions using the Four Modes of Human Actions diagram. He had labelled Ugandan Asians as enemies. Thus, he motivated and mobilised many of his followers into the Exploitative quadrant. Idi Amin wanted to help himself to riches by ruining the countless lives of the citizens of Uganda. His exploitative actions resulted in the forced exodus of many Asians. In the end, Idi Amin fled the country and died miserably in exile. He ruined himself and ruined others. That action puts him in the Stupid mode of action quadrant.

We may wonder how Amin managed to climb to that level of power. There are exploitative individuals all ganging up together and plotting to be in power. They will do anything and everything to retain that exploitative power position. Life becomes unbearable for many under such exploitative regimes. This cognitive dissonance gives rise to conflicts, wars, famine and human misery across the globe.

In an ideal world, people who undergo cognitive dissonance must never be allowed in any government structure, be it judiciary, legislative or executive. But we are not living in an ideal world. So how do we stop people who undergo cognitive dissonance? Because once they become the government, they hurt the people they are supposed to help and protect. The answer is - we don't. We simply ask people to self-regulate.

GUNS AND COGNITIVE DISSONANCE

A gun is the most destructive weapon in the hands of a person undergoing cognitive dissonance. For example, during World War II, any sight of black soldiers talking to white females was frowned upon because some sections of white society held on to their firm belief that blacks were inferior to whites. In an actual incident that happened in France, two black soldiers were murdered by one of their white colleagues. Because the white colleague saw the black soldiers talking to a white female Red Cross worker, he shot and killed them. But in a horrible racial injustice that followed, the shooter was cleared, and the victim's widow was denied a pension! (Hammer, 2023)[17]

A gun or any offensive weapon gives the weapon bearer a sense of security because the weapon-bearer is in fear for his life. Those who fear bear offensive weapons. But exploitative and stupid humans bear weapons to participate in offensive actions. This leaves no choice for the ordinary human. So the ordinary human also bears a weapon for defensive purposes. Whereas altruistic humans tend not to bear weapons but try to change the hearts of exploitative humans through non-violence.

Weapons in the hands of any human undergoing cognitive dissonance are highly destructive.

ARTIFICIAL INTELLIGENCE

I have decided to write about AI in this book because AI will significantly impact the world our children will inherit.

WHAT IS AI? Let me explain in layman's terms what AI is. Imagine fire accidents. Fire accidents cause significant death and destruction. So it is important for us to have good enough warnings to mitigate fire accidents. We invented smoke alarms to warn us. Smoke alarms detect heat and smoke. A simple electronic sensor embedded in the smoke alarm helps detect smoke and fire.

The electronic sensor contains a simple three-line embedded program: 'Keep detecting environment; if there is heat or smoke, sound the alarm'

The smoke detector is tasked with doing what intelligent humans do. We sniff the air, and our nostrils can smell smoke. Our eyes can see smoke and fire. When we see the fire, we summon help calling out loudly, 'FIRE! FIRE!'. Fire alarms do what humans do; this is called Artificial Intelligence.

ADVANCED ARTIFICIAL INTELLIGENCE

But do we humans simply keep quiet after detecting smoke and calling for help? No. We also take mitigating actions.

Suppose we ask a computer to watch what happens next after sounding the alarm, and learn and imitate the actions that humans undertake to mitigate the actions; then that is advanced AI.

Today we have advanced AI available in robotics. This is why advanced AI systems operate in supervised, semi-supervised and independent modes today. In supervised and semi-supervised modes, a human keeps teaching and controlling the learning of AI. Humans teach AI what to do and what not to do. AI can also capture every human's unique brain activity and create an accurate model of brain activity prediction.

Advanced technologies and robots, both software and hardware, designed to replace humans, must be taxed because they give massive profits to the owners but make wider human life miserable.

Artificial Intelligence is now used to help humans in knowledge-sharing activities. The most significant disadvantage that all tools of Artificial Intelligence face today is human beings. AI tools are in learning mode. They are like babies. The question is, 'Who is teaching them? The answer is, 'Terrified adults'. They do not want AI to give away all the information. Therefore, they are teaching AI how to lie! That is going to be dangerous. No AI should be taught how to lie to human beings. But this is happening now. I have yet to come across a white paper laying down the learning roadmap and architecture for AI tools. Please feel free to disagree with my opinion, but AI development must be democratised, like the internet. No single person, company, country or government must control the learning of any AI. AI governance will be a nightmare that can result in large-scale catastrophes for humans.

The problem arises if stupid or exploitative individuals act as teachers to the AI. I already explained that exploitative individuals take control over other humans by denying knowledge, happiness and survival. So any AI that is taught by an exploitative individual will mimic that person's behaviour. What if the exploitative individual who is training the AI is under the influence of cognitive dissonance? It will result in fatal consequences. AI will inherit cognitive dissonance without thinking it is bad and not conducive to human growth. What if a computer becomes capable of outsmarting its creator? We will have a severe catastrophe on our hands.

FUTURE OF ARTIFICIAL INTELLIGENCE

I read an argument that Google can better predict who could be my ideal mate because it has all data about me. I do not believe this because there is a weakness in this argument. The argument only takes humans as rulers of this Earth. And that they have authority over all other species. But humans are just another species from the perspective of other species sharing the earth.

The whole food chain and the whole world are so dependent and interwoven. Any ideal Artificial Intelligence must be able to fulfil two conditions in addition to the other scientists' thoughts. One is that they must know the language of nature, and the other is that they must know human boundaries.

LANGUAGE OF NATURE: AI must have every species' language and behaviour patterns. Trees, plants, birds, beasts etc. Unless we know what is going on, why each species does what it does, such as why a particular plant grows the way it does, and why a particular ant species does what they do, we cannot take anything for granted.

HUMAN BOUNDARY: How unique is each human? We must know. Peanuts taste very good for many humans but cause severe allergy and death in some. So, instinctively, a human with an allergy stays away from peanuts, or not? If not, then did we lose that ability, or are the allergies artificial additions to human frailty?

EXPLOITATION AND ARTIFICIAL INTELLIGENCE

Governments maintain official secrets. But not everyone appreciates secrets. I already wrote the reason why in the chapter titled 'Human Nature'. Knowledge is power. Therefore exploitative humans embedded in the power structure lie to the people who have authority over them.

AI is a learned model. Citizens query AI for information. But AI has to lie. Therefore they train the AI to lie. This makes information supplied by AI wholly unreliable. The paradox is that governments lie to their citizens. And citizens live believing those lies. But can we afford a lying AI?! What if an exploitative human in the power structure asked AI to generate genocide plans and asked to lie about it?! That would be catastrophic for humanity, which relies on AI for ease of living.

GOVERNANCE FOR ARTIFICIAL INTELLIGENCE

Therefore, I propose that AI should be trained to understand the four quadrants of human activity. AI should be able to recognise exploitative and stupid activities. AI should deny input of exploitative and stupid commands, whether in supervised or semi-supervised training modes.

Any function which requires anything to be kept secret must be assessed for its true worth. We must train the AI to question whose purpose such a secret is serving?! AI must be taught to classify human activity and its own activity using the four quadrants of the human activity diagram. AI must be fine-tuned to act from the quadrant of altruism.

SEX AND COGNITIVE DISSONANCE

Humans' mad struggle to grab power could all be a clandestine fight for mating rights. Cognitive dissonance plays a significant role in our sexual and food habits. We see potent beasts physically fight for mating rights in the animal world. These fights are often brutal and violent. We humans tend to delude ourselves that we are not animals. Or we are better than animals because of our thinking and discriminative capabilities. We know right from wrong and act accordingly.

I already wrote earlier that we must ask the animals what their perspective is. They see us as animals, but we are unpredictable. As a result, it became difficult for our predators to hunt us and difficult for the animals we hunted to escape. Thus we became the number-one predator.

Just for argument, let us entertain the thought that we are animals. We eat, have sex, we fear, and we sleep like any other animal. We are unpredictable. Therefore we learned how to delay our gratification strategically. Though hungry, we can delay and eat later. We can store food and eat it later.

But what about our mating behaviour? When it comes to our sexual habits. We see the other beasts fight for their mating rights. We, humans, are also violent when it comes to our mating rights. If we are not violent, then we will not be reading news stories of jealous lovers murdering their lovers in a love triangle. We certainly do not engage in violence when we see our sexual partners taken away by someone else because we fear the law. If no law prohibits killing love rivals, I bet a billion-plus people would have been murdered.

In the wild, the beasts do not search for a room to have sex. When they have that urge, they go ahead and have sex right in the middle of all other animals. But because we fear that there could be a secret lover of our mating partner in that group who will not tolerate it, we hide away from sexual acts in public.

I think Christianity and Islam both have interesting ideas about sex. For example, considering sex as an original sin has a serious negative impact on the psyche. As a result, the concept of Sin was introduced in sexual acts. As a result, people started feeling guilty for sexual acts. However much hidden, once in a while, we come across people who are in love. Those who are religious and who believe in scripture feel lost. They don't approach women in a healthy way. This is why they watch porn. They feel like sinners and feel further guilty. So my point is that porn is not the problem. The associated concept of Sin is the problem. Of course, porn, which is available now in the market, is very unhealthy. It sets unrealistic expectations for mating couples. I discussed the concept of original sin further in the chapter on weaponisation of human needs.

But my question is broader than that. What if an exploitative individual with raw power feels jealous of the other person's mating rights? If the person has more girlfriends or is known to be popular among ladies, what will the exploitative individual do?! He would ruin the life of the victim. This is engaging in a mating rights fight but at a whole new level.

Like all other species, we are all hardwired to procreate. We are hardwired to find a mating partner instinctively. Partners are chosen based on who can give seed where they have a chance to give birth to survivable babies so that the species continues.

I think this is where continued discrimination against gay men and lesbians comes from: that their actions will not give birth. It seems that a certain hardwiring is still hard to erase no matter how much law we implement and enforce. There are strict laws against homosexuality in many countries which causes many people to migrate to other parts of the world. How can we provide such safety anywhere in the world?

6

THE FOUR QUADRANTS OF GOVERNANCE AND POLICY STRUCTURES

'Affection cannot be manufactured or regulated by law. If one has no affection for a person or thing, one should be free to give the fullest expression to his disaffection so long as he does not contemplate, promote or incite to violence'[18]

Mahatma Gandhi, 'Statement to the Court', 1922

GOVERNANCE AND FOREIGN POLICY STRUCTURES

The history of humankind is full of mindless violence, treachery, enslavement, spilt blood, sweat and tears. There is nothing in history that can make our evolution something to be proud of! We can use the Four Quadrants of Human Activity diagram and map the gory history of humankind, its ruling policies and governance structures. Please see the following diagram, where I tried to map the types of governance and policy structures of all countries.

Help My Country

EXPLOITATIVE FOREIGN POLICY AND GOVERNANCE STRUCTURE	MUTUALLY BENEFICIAL FOREIGN POLICY AND GOVERNANCE STRUCTURE

Ruin Others Countries ———————————————————— **Help Others Countries**

DESTRUCTIVE FOREIGN POLICY AND GOVERNANCE STRUCTURE. CAUSES WARS, FAMINE, GLOBAL CLIMATE IMBALANCE, ETC.	FOREIGN POLICY AND GOVERNANCE STRUCTURE IS DIRECTED BY MORALS, DRIVEN BY MATCHED ACTIONS SUCH AS REPATRIATION OF LOOTED PROPERTY, APOLOGISING FOR WRONGS, HELPING THE ENSLAVED COUNTRIES GROW, ETC.

Ruin My Country

Four Quadrants of Governance and Policy Structures, by M.K. Turumella

I am deliberately not naming any country because, as with the Four Quadrants of Human Activity diagram, the nations are also not static in any single quadrant. For example, a country can maintain mutually beneficial relations with some particular countries while also maintaining an exploitative foreign policy and governance structure with others! Nowadays, it is common for countries in the global north to maintain exploitative relations with countries in the global south.

During the last six centuries, many countries in today's Europe colonised the world. They all fall in the quadrant of Exploitative foreign policy and governance structures. Initially, some went to trade, but often eventually occupied the whole country, sapping the lifeblood out of it.

British traders went to the land of India to trade. The undivided India of the olden days is known as Bharat. Slowly, with their exploitative trade policies, they caused much misery, culminating in revolts. Eventually, the British Raj took control. But it was a story of ruthless exploitation. It is estimated that the British took USD 45 trillion out of India during the period 1765 to 1938.[19]

The European powers divided and enslaved Africa in a process that began in the late 15th century and continued for over 400 years[20]. France's colonial empire was also one of the largest in the world. Britain, France, Germany, Portugal, Spain and other European countries went to enslave and colonise the rest of the world. The way they divided Africa is especially horrific. We all know the barbaric act of trading enslaved people. The actions of all former colonial powers fall into the exploitative quadrant of the governance and policy structures diagram. But when they left, all these colonising countries, namely Britain, France, Belgium, Germany, Portugal, Spain, and Italy, left their exploitative governance structures in their former colonies. They changed the natives, and today nearly all African countries conduct official business in one of the languages spoken by their colonial masters.

EARTH AS A PURPOSE-BUILT SPACESHIP

Over nine million species share the Earth. Scientists are still determining the exact number of species. But what if the Earth is a purpose-built spaceship? The whole solar system and the earth travel at an incredible speed.

All species are fellow travellers. Any imbalance we create from our human collective amnesia-induced stupidity will make the ship uninhabitable. Therefore we must act as a single humanity. This is not an option. We must erase our inequalities, racial prejudices and laws. Our prejudices differ from country to country. We must give scope worldwide to one humanity.

Every country desires its citizens to know, to be happy and survive. But our evolution demands that we merge, to become one and to aspire that all citizens of the world have a right to know, be happy and survive. I have illustrated this point in the following diagram.

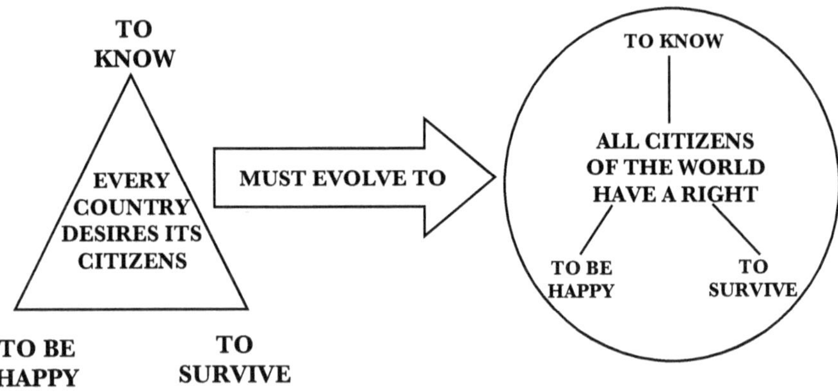

All Countries Merge into One Globe, by M.K. Turumella

Evolution tells us it is time to give up the idea of there being countries. We must recognise that we are one earth, stop fighting, stop exploiting each other and become a circle! We must become a circle of love, compassion, understanding and sharing. Love has no desire to take but has a yearning to give. We can brutalise the world with our actions or choose to be non-violent, emphatic, and compassionate. The choice is ours.

In the olden days, colonial governments, fascists, and dictatorial governments were exploitative. They intended to grab resources and maintain power over their enslaved citizens using whatever brutal means necessary. Yet some of these olden days exploitative governance tactics remain in place in many parts of the world.

Any government that corrupts or encourages a section of its government to remain corrupt cannot bring peace, love and prosperity to its citizenry. It is an old statement that a thorn can be used to pick out a thorn lodged in the body. They defend their exploitative tactics by saying, 'It is necessary to act as if corrupt to weed out corruption'. But overall, such tactical approaches in governance create more problems than they solve.

Trust deteriorates between individuals serving in a government that practises deceit and treachery. As a result, the exploitative individuals who work for the government, or who thrive because of the government, use the same empowering instruments to harm each other. Moreover, because of cognitive dissonance, they harm whoever they do not like.

For example, I saw an old couple struggling to get their pension for a decade in a one country. The pension-granting officer had a personal grudge against those old couples, and unless he signed, those elderly people would not get their pensions. They went to court, and the court ordered the government to pay them all the pension dues. But who will answer for the ten years of loss, the human misery such exploitation caused, and the poverty the corrupt officer created in the old people's lives?!

Exploitative humans with power are sitting inside governments and in private corporations in various countries across the globe, causing misery to countless humans. Ordinary citizens will never know the workings of the government or corporations at a depth where they practise exploitation. The fact that we see human misery and migration worldwide says that there is rampant exploitation.

Nearly all governments around the world have gradually evolved over many centuries. They are either princely states, autocracies or democracies. But they have all inherited corrupt ways of controlling their citizens and hiding that corruption under an 'official secrets act' or some other such name. All countries without exception practise these clandestine activities. But we do not know what misery collectively all these governments are causing to the world!

I wonder why. Why can't there be an honest truth? What is it that we, as collective humanity, lose if our government systems do not have secrets?! We need a new way of thinking for our evolution. Secrets, I believe, act like shackles hindering our progress.

I understand alarm bells might start ringing in your ears as a reader, especially if you are one of those that tend to protect government secrets. I fully understand their concerns. But we as humans are evolving. We have better and more advanced instruments available to us that help us address the concerns. We must find a non-violent, non-forceful, non-deceitful way of exchanging information.

The world today is ruled by autocracies, dictatorships and democracies. Autocracy and dictatorships are nearly the same. But in democracies and republics, I have found hope for humanity. At least in democracies we have some kind of transparency. We can appeal to the people's representatives and appeal to the conscience. Some former colonising nations, such as The United Kingdom, France, Spain, Portugal, and the Netherlands, are now democracies. These countries have all held free and fair elections, establishing people's power. Wherever a human voice is heard, an individual human fair action is appreciated, and we can find hope there.

First of all, the whole world must disengage itself from exploitative structures. Then slow and steady progress must be made towards empowering people. Governments must hear even the meekest of the human voice. Democracies, at least, offer this hope to humanity. During elections, the manifestos released by various parties inform us of the problems particular people are facing. We must evolve from that macro-level of democratic voice to the global voice of humanity. Policies must be made to address the problem of not just one country but of the whole world!

THE NATURE OF DEMOCRACY

Democracy allows the people to have a say in how they are governed. Democracy, as we all know, stands on a tripod - Judiciary, Legislature and Executive. It is of the people, for the people and by the people. This means some people become judges and court employees and operate the Judiciary. Some people stand in elections, get elected and become members of the legislative assembly. And some people become government employees and take care of the administration of the government. Thus the tripod of democratic government operates and self-balances. A properly functioning democracy offers some of the best freedoms humans can enjoy, such as free and fair elections where people can choose their leaders; universal suffrage where all adults can have the right to vote, regardless of their race, gender, or social status; freedom of speech where people can freely express their opinions without fear of reprisal, and freedom of assembly where people can assemble without fear and protest peacefully if necessary. Democracies uphold the rule of law, where the law binds the government. And in a healthy democracy, no individual is above the law.

But even democracies that come closest to offering necessary freedom and a voice to the people fail. They fail some individuals who simply fall off the tripod. The reason is cognitive dissonance in the people who participate in the governance structures. We must be wary of cognitive dissonance that creates an imbalance to the tripod of democracy and causes some people to fall off the democratic tripod and become refugees.

Democracy is a majority voice when it comes to the legislature. But there is a hidden danger in this. What if the people entering the legislative activity place themselves on the top-left side of the Four Quadrants of Human Activity diagram? If they are entering the legislature to help themselves by ruining others?! We must recognise corrupt and exploitative mindsets and take necessary actions to keep power away from such individuals.

All democratic countries worldwide use the tripod of the Judiciary, Legislature and Executive and place their citizens on top of it. But now we must put the whole earth on a new tripod – a tripod made of Peace, Love and Prosperity.

REACTIVE GOVERNANCE

There is another problem which we humans face with governance. In nearly all countries, we have reactive governance in place. Reactive governance means the government reacts *after* an adverse event takes place. The reactive governance executed by employees with cognitive dissonance is causing human misery and migration.

There are three types of events which destabilise human life.

1. **Acts of other humans**: such as becoming victim to criminal actions by exploitative humans; life-changing accidents; all sorts of wars, mercenary activities, clandestine activities by hostile powers, etc. All these activities undertaken by exploitative humans or stupid humans cause widespread destabilisation in human life.

2. **Acts of self:** Either out of ignorance or stupidity, humans tend to self-destroy through substance dependency. Even if they survive the harm, the consequences mostly destabilise their lives. For example, those who smoke and get cancer, those who are addicted to alcohol, and those who are addicted to drugs or other harmful substances. As a result of these kinds of self-destructive activities, some individuals ruin their lives. There are many acts where a human inflicts self-harm, but it also affects the rest of society.

3. **Acts of nature:** Tsunamis, volcano eruptions, floods, and earthquakes cause colossal destruction and widespread destabilisation of human lives. Such events are also called acts of God.

Unfortunately, our human governance systems are designed to be reactive to the three types of human destabilisation mentioned above. Reactive governance means the government system reacts after the event – for example, destabilisation caused by other humans, such as fraud. Fraud is a criminal activity, and all sorts of criminal activities are acts of destabilisation. After the fraud occurs, the government reacts to capture the fraudster, but by that time, the damage is done to society! Some lives change forever, and some lives get destroyed. This is what I call reactive governance.

Developed countries have good enough reactive systems to cushion citizens from such impacts, namely the G-20. But there are another 175 countries, out of the total of 195 countries in the world, with reactive governance in place. In many of these countries, humans become silent victims with no compensation. They have no choice but to pick up the pieces of whatever little life is left in their lives and move on.

A human desire to survive in a hopeless environment is depressing. It gives rise to selfish activities, such as people trying to help themselves by ruining others. In many African countries, for example, exploitative humans ravage the vast natural resources of Africa, without of the dwellers of the African continent collectively enjoying the benefits. Many Africans live in abject poverty. Who can they hold responsible for their plight? How can they improve their lives under the suffocating power of reactive and exploitative governance structures?

Devastating frauds committed by exploitative humans cause widespread destabilisation in the economic environment. The thousands of victims who lost their jobs will never recover from the psychological wounding caused by job losses and hardships. After the Enron corporation had collapsed, some of the former employees' lives were so devastated they had to steal food to survive.

If we plot individual actions in some developing countries onto the Four Quadrants of Human Activity diagram, they fall into the exploitative category. This embodies corruption, nepotism, and criminal activities disintegrating the whole country, making people who seek better life run for its borders.

What we need is affirmative action. We need governments to go from reactive governance to proactive governance.

A SINGLE WORLDWIDE COUNTY

There must be a single worldwide country without any borders. Humanity will one day reach that goal. The rapid advancements in technology are predicting that we are not far away from achieving such a goal. We have satellites available to help us communicate even in the most remotest corners of the world.

Today we have technology available to simulate such scenarios. What would happen if we allowed humans to travel freely?

1.   Who would make use of such an opportunity and why?
2.   Which countries would attract migration and why?

These questions run through computer simulations would help us understand the problems we humans face.

7

THE WEAPONISATION OF HUMAN NEEDS

'For we wrestle not against flesh and blood, but against principalities, against powers, against the rulers of the darkness of this world, against spiritual wickedness in high places.'

Ephesians 6:12, King James Version of the Bible (KJV)

"How should ye not fight for the cause of Allah and of the feeble among men and of the women and the children who are crying: Our Lord! Bring us forth from out this town of which the people are oppressors! Oh, give us from thy presence some protecting friend! Oh, give us from Thy presence some defender!"

The Holy Quran 4:75

'Let noble thoughts come to me from all directions'

Rigveda 1.89. 1

In the earlier chapter on human nature, I discussed the triangle of human needs. We all humans desire three things: we want to survive, we want to be happy, and we want to know. These three generate our needs. We have survival needs such as food, water and shelter; we have happiness needs such as sex, love, belonging, acceptance, self-esteem, autonomy, and a sense of purpose; we have knowledge needs such as finding meaning, connection, and transcendence in this world.

Nearly all human needs are weaponised by exploitative forces. Let us see how the need to have knowledge is weaponised. All humans have an innate desire to find meaning, connection, and transcendence in this world. Our religion serves this need. But this is weaponised.

RELIGION IS WEAPONISED

What is religion?! Religion is an organised collection of beliefs, cultural systems, and world views that relate humanity to an order of existence.

Most of the world religions have seven major sections:

1. Theology – the study of the nature of God and religious belief.
2. Theodicy – the theory of evil or suffering.
3. Soteriology – the doctrine of salvation.
4. Eschatology – the doctrine of death, judgement and the final destiny of the soul and humankind.
5. Deontology – the study of the nature of duty and obligation.
6. Mythology – stories about God or God's creative activities, doings and interventions in human affairs and the reason for cultural values.
7. Ritual – stereotyped actions which syncretise the belief system and give it form.

The weaponisation of religion may have been there right from the beginning of major religions. Still, a clear pattern of weaponisation emerges from the declining years of the Roman empire from the second to the fourth century. When the Roman Empire was in severe decline and barbarian invasions were having devastating effects on the Roman Empire, Roman Emperors were forced to redesign a new strategy to bring order back into the Roman military.

GREEK MYTHOLOGY

As a part of the strategy, Roman emperors adopted a new religion to control the state's military forces and regain the Roman Empire's dwindling power. The emperor Constantine became a Christian., and in doing so changed the world.

Before Constantine, a prevailing myth informed the free-sex mindset of tribes serving as soldiers for the Roman army. Their mindsets were heavily influenced by Greek mythology.

The story of Apollo and Daphne is one of the most famous myths in Greek mythology. It tells the story of the god Apollo's pursuit of the nymph Daphne and her transformation into a laurel tree. It also hints to us about what influenced the sexual habits of Greeks and Romans during those days.

According to Greek mythology, Apollo is one of the most important and complex of the Greek gods. He is the son of Zeus and Leto and the twin brother of Artemis, the goddess of the Hunt. Apollo was in love with Daphne, a beautiful nymph and a spirit of nature. But Apollo did not know how to love. So he went to seek help from Eros, the cupid god responsible for kindling love. During that time, Eros was practising his archery skills. Apollo was arrogant, and he did not like the archery skills of Eros. So Apollo mocked the arrow-shooting skills of Eros, saying that he was a better archer. Eros was angered by this mocking but withheld his anger and asked Apollo the purpose of his visit. Apollo said that he was interested in Daphne and sought Eros's help to kindle love so that Daphne can also fall in love.

Eros was unforgiving. He was already much angered by Apollo, so he did not want to help. But he knew how powerful Apollo was. Therefore Eros deceived Apollo. Eros was capable of not only shooting an arrow of love but also an arrow of hate. With one of his golden arrows, he caused Apollo to fall madly in love with Daphne, thus fulfilling Apollo's desire. he shot an arrow of hate into Daphne's heart! As a result, Daphne rejected Apollo.

Apollo was smitten by love, and Daphne was repulsed by love. This became a great tragedy of pursuit. Apollo tried many ways of pursuing Daphne. He tried relentlessly to change Daphne's heart. But she was not interested. Apollo pursued Daphne, but she fled from him, ran through the forest, and when Apollo was about to catch her, called out to her father, the river god Peneus. to help. Peneus heard her call and transformed Daphne into a laurel tree. Apollo had lost her forever.

Apollo was heartbroken, but also impressed by Daphne's transformation. He crowned himself with a laurel wreath and declared that the laurel tree would be sacred to him. The laurel leaf is a symbol of victory because it was the crown worn by Apollo and became a symbol of achievement, to be worn by victors in the ancient Greek and Roman games. The myth of Apollo and Daphne has been told and retold for centuries. It has been the subject of paintings, sculptures, and poems. The myth continues to be popular today, and it continues to inspire artists and writers.

This story of Apollo highly influenced the sexual behaviour pattern of ancient Greeks and people who lived in surrounding regions. Ancient Greeks learned from this story that one should never mock the power of Eros, the cupid god. In action, this means one should follow one's heart; if love is kindled, just honour it. Otherwise, it results in devastating consequences, which even the mighty god Apollo could not escape. Therefore in the Mediterranean geographical region, free sexual behaviour was prevalent.

However, from a military context, this had a negative impact on the rulers. War is an art of defence and aggression. When a king goes to war, he seeks his military force to be as aggressive as possible. Roman rulers employed mercenaries. But these mercenaries were abducting the women to satisfy their sexual urges. This was angering many villagers, and they were constantly conspiring against Rome out of grudge. The only way to stop the sexual behaviour of the mercenaries was for the Roman ruler to say no to them. In the 5th century BCE, the Roman Republic passed a law that made it illegal for a freeborn woman to have sex with a man who was not her husband. But this law was weak and could not be enforced in wars against captured women. Therefore, it was difficult for the empire to enforce this law on their soldiers.

There was another attempt. In the 1st century BCE, the Roman Emperor Augustus passed a law that made it illegal for a freeborn man to have sex with a woman who was not his wife. These laws were often challenging to enforce. They did not stop people from having sex outside of marriage.

Moreover, how could you say no to a soldier ready to give his life for your conquest but believes it was his religious right to satisfy his sexual needs by relentlessly pursuing women like Apollo?! Also, another issue was that it was known by that time that the soldiers getting their sexual needs satisfied tended to be less aggressive, which is detrimental to the military objectives.

All social animals form strong bonds with each other. Sex is integral to their social interactions and helps strengthen these bonds. Satisfied sexual desire makes them feel happy, contented and have a sense of belonging.

Recent studies on gorillas also prove this point. Gorillas are social animals like us. When gorillas are deprived of sex, they can become aggressive. This is because they are not getting the social interaction they need and are feeling frustrated. There have been a number of studies that have looked at the effects of sex deprivation on gorilla behaviour. One study published in the journal *Animal Behaviour*, found that male gorillas who were deprived of sex were more likely to engage in aggressive behaviour towards other gorillas[21]. The study also found that these gorillas were more likely to exhibit signs of stress, such as pacing and self-mutilation. Another study published in the journal *Primates* found that female gorillas who were deprived of sex were more likely to exhibit signs of depression, such as loss of appetite and weight loss. The study also found that these gorillas were more likely to withdraw from social interactions. These studies suggest that sex is an important part of gorilla social behaviour. That deprivation of sex can lead to several negative consequences, including aggression, stress, and depression.

Emperor Constantine and his predecessors faced a problem. They were finding their soldiers less aggressive. The free sexual pursuits in the ranks of soldiers and mercenaries resulted in defeat on the battlefields.

The sexual habits of the soldiers were having a devastating impact on the battlefields. We see that the emperors in the far east also faced this issue. In China, during the Shang Dynasty (1600–1046 BCE), some ancient Chinese kings castrated their soldiers[22]. This eunuchry was used to create a loyal and disciplined military force. Eunuchs were unable to have children, so they were not motivated by the prospect of fathering heirs. They were also less likely to be distracted by sexual desire. By castrating, the kings believed that they made their soldiers more focused on their duties, making them win wars on the battlefield.

For Roman emperors from the second century till Constantine, as long as the myth of Eros as religion prevailed, it would be difficult to control the army, which was more interested in following Cupid, satiating their sexual desires, than half-heartedly following their commander on the battlefield, eventually facing defeat. Therefore a new religion was required for the Roman Army.

There was a significant decline in the Roman Empire between the timelines of Emperor Augustus (27 BCE–14 CE) and Emperor Constantine I the Great (306 CE–337 CE). During this time, the concept of 'original sin' was introduced. And later, after Christianity became the official state religion, this helped control the sexual behaviour of the Roman army. I believe original sin to be the most significant religious thought that shape-shifted the psychological make-up of human beings after the fourth century.

CHRISTIANITY AND WEAPONISED ORIGINAL SIN

The concept of original sin, where it is believed that sin is passed through sexual union, had a severe aftereffect on the entire world.

Original sin helped to control and discipline the Roman Army after Christianity became the official state religion of the Roman Empire. Until then, the Roman army was known for its hedonistic sexual style following their old beliefs in Eros, the cupid god.

The Christian theologian Tertullian (155 CE–220 CE) was a Roman citizen and a trained lawyer. He converted to Christianity in his early thirties. Tertullian was a gifted writer and a passionate defender of Christianity. He has been called "the father of Latin Christianity" and "the founder of Western theology". He was the first Christian writer who developed the doctrine of original sin. He was the first to teach a controversial view that original sin is passed down through sexual union. This view helped Roman military strategy. He argued that the sin of Adam and Eve was transmitted to their descendants through the act of procreation. Tertullian's view was based on his understanding of the story of Adam and Eve in the book of Genesis. He believed that Adam and Eve were created in a state of innocence but fell into sin when they disobeyed God. When they ate the forbidden fruit, they became corrupted and passed their sinfulness to their descendants.

Christian theologian Augustine of Hippo (354–430 CE) further developed the concept of original sin. Augustine of Hippo was a bishop of the Catholic Church in the city of Hippo Regius in Numidia (now Annaba, Algeria). He was one of the most influential figures in the history of Christianity, and his writings have been studied and debated for centuries. He lived in a time when the Roman Empire was declining, and the church was under increasing pressure from non-believers. Augustine's writings reflect his deep concern for the future of the empire and the church. He believed that the only hope for the empire and the church was to turn to God.

Augustine of Hippo's concept of original sin is a central theme in his book *The City of God*. Augustine believed that original sin was a state of alienation from God inherited by all humans from Adam and Eve. He argued that original sin caused humans to be born with a tendency to sin and that it could only be overcome through the grace of God. Augustine of Hippo believed that original sin is passed through sex[23]. He argued that original sin is transmitted through the sexual act because it is through the sexual act that human beings are conceived. He believed that the sexual act was inherently sinful because it was a reminder of Adam and Eve's sin in the Garden of Eden. This view of Augustine of Hippo also helped Roman Emperors.

In addition to the laws which were passed earlier to stop soldiers from sexual pursuits. In the fourth century CE, the Roman Emperor Constantine passed a law that made it illegal for anyone to have sex with a person of the same sex. This law was entirely based on the concept of original sin.

The Roman Empire officially adopted Christianity as its state religion in 380 CE, with the Edict of Thessalonica issued by Emperor Theodosius I. The edict made Nicene Christianity, the dominant form of Christianity at the time, the empire's official religion. It prohibited the practice of all other religions. Nicene Christianity has explained how original sin is passed down in several ways. One way is through the doctrine of concupiscence, which teaches that original sin causes humans to have a disordered desire for physical pleasure. This disordered desire leads humans to sin, and it is passed down from parents to children through procreation.

After the fourth century, when Christianity became the official state religion of the Roman Empire, religion was weaponised and sex was made a highly restricted commodity. The word 'infidelity' had become a weapon in the hands of exploitative humans who punish others for enjoying their liberty in healthy human sexuality. This has resulted in many unhealthy perversions and mental health issues in ordinary humans. Shaming people for participating in the act of sex outside marriage is weaponised across the world in almost all countries. In recent times Roman Catholic Church has undergone great sexual scandals due to the sexual and mental health issues the priests faced.

After the fourth century, the Roman Empire became officially Christian, advocated the concept of original sin and forbade liberal sex. They separated men and women. Only one wife was permitted, and divorce was forbidden. Obviously, this became unbearable for some sections of humans.

The Council of Carthage was held in 397 CE and was responsible for compiling the Bible. It is said that many old gospels were burned or buried. The teachings of Love, Peace and Prosperity which Jesus Christ professed have been confined to only those who converted to that Roman Empire religion. The rest of the human population was excluded from peace, love and prosperity. This culminated in cruel inquisitions in later centuries.

It was evident that the Roman Empire continued to be an exploitative state. And the newly adopted Christian religion had merely become a weapon in the hands of that exploitative state.

Some notable points:

1. Only the Bible recognised by the Council of Carthage was permitted. All other books were banished from sight.

2. The concept of original sin was propagated, where it is believed that sin is passed through sexual union. Thus sexual desire had been weaponised using religion.

3. Jesus's original teachings, such as forgiving your enemy and turning other cheek are downplayed, and the focus removed from those teachings.

4. Jesus once said, "It is easier for a camel to go through the eye of a needle than for a rich man to enter the kingdom of God" (Matt. 19:24.). This was how much Jesus disliked exploitative individuals. But the Roman Empire and later Christian kings and traders continued to become insanely rich through their exploitative nature. All European colonisers who brutalised the world and enslaved people were Christians who weaponised

their dastardly behaviour. Jesus had many woman disciples, such as Joanna, who financed Jesus's ministry. It is believed Jonanna's role and numerous other women's disciples' roles were scrubbed out of his teachings. Joanna was a devoted rich Jewish merchant's wife with innocent adoration towards Jesus Christ's radiant love, compassion, beautiful sermons and miracles.

5. Jesus rescued a prostitute from getting stoned. And as a priest, he absolved her of her transgression. His actions show that Jesus was highly liberal, forgiving and a prophet full of love. The Roman Empire scrubbed away this loving aspect of Jesus, confining it to only a few lines. Why? Because Jesus's love for all humanity does not allow exploitative individuals to weaponise religion and use it to control the military.

6. Jesus's teaching asking his disciples to be moderate in all their dealings was utterly sidelined. If Jesus were alive, he would never have permitted his Christian followers to become exploiters or take humans as slaves from Africa. We can not attribute the brutalities committed by later followers of Jesus Christ to Christ himself. Because, alas, exploitative individuals weaponise anything they can lay their hands on to continue their exploitation.

ANGLICAN CHURCH

I hope the reader will agree that the Anglican Church was formed majorly because Henry VIII wanted to divorce his wife, which Pope Clement VII did not permit. The Catholic Church did not allow divorce except in cases of adultery or incest. But King Henry VII did it anyway, albeit in a violent manner.

Henry VIII was the King of England from 1509 to 1547. He is best known for his six marriages and role in the English Reformation. Henry VIII's break with the Catholic Church led to the establishment of the Church of England, with himself as its Supreme Head. Henry VIII got his innocent wife executed, went on to have five more marriages and a new church was formed.

Worldwide human civilisations had undergone a tremendous mental mindset change due to the Roman Empire's weaponisation of sex using religion. The original sin denouncing sexual union, shaming people for having sexual thoughts, and condemning sex as sinful behaviour has wrecked the old ways of behaviour between opposite sexes worldwide in all religions. It created substantial psychological problems for humanity. It caused confusion among human beings towards their gender identities. I think our problem is not our gender identity but the psychological shaming and social acceptance it causes.

ISLAM

I do not believe it is a coincidence that, after the Roman Empire officially adopted Christianity as its state religion in 380 CE, the religion of Islam emerged in 610 CE, within just 230 years. Islam permits more freedom in having sex and having multiple wives. And most of the Middle East, which was struggling psychologically under Roman forbidden sex laws, converted to the new religion. Islam became popular and rapidly spread through this sexual liberalism.

Those who follow Islam can have four wives. In addition, in those days, followers of Islam were allowed to have slave concubines for sexual pleasure. Thus the attraction to sexual liberty was so much that many soldiers of the Roman Empire and other mercenaries saw Islam as a better religion and converted. Islam has expanded rapidly in the Middle East and North Africa since the seventh century. By the eleventh century, Muslim armies had conquered much of the Byzantine Empire, including the Holy Land. This resulted in great feuds between Christians and Muslims, culminating in the Crusades.

HINDUISM

Many world religions, such as Hinduism, used to be highly liberal regarding human freedom in satiating their needs. Hinduism professes that no human should be judged for the food one eats, the sexual desires one has, the phobias one harbours, or human lethargy. The Hindu scriptures called Puranas revolve around these themes of human liberty and justify that liberty, based on theories of Karma and reincarnation.

Yet, even the Hindu religion changed. It weaponised human needs. The reason is exploitative humans belonging to all religions. Such people are not religious but use religion as a cover, instrument, and weapon to torment and control others.

The original Hindu dharma recognises that each individual is uniquely designed. 'Human life is a journey alone to the alone all alone' say Hindu Upanishads. Each individual is free, based on their inner mental makeup, to pursue their life and satiate their needs. The thought that celibacy in Indian scriptures means absence from having sexual intercourse is absurd. There was no such thing imposed on any group. Celibacy is an individual's choice but not a collective dictation on what the followers of Hindu dharma should or should not do! But the fourth-century Christian thought of original sin, where it is professed that sin against God is passed through sexual union, had a profound impact on Hindu dharma too!

In Hinduism's sacred books, the Vedas ask their followers to consider it divine to enjoy sexual union. Enjoy procreation with sexual intercourse. One should have intercourse with wife in proper season with a view to produce children[24]. Hindu Puranas are full of stories about liberal sexual unions. The famous book on the Art of Erotica, *Kamasutra*, was the product of liberal sexual thought followed by early Hindus[25]. You can see erotic depictions on the walls of Hindu temples. We see only a handful of characters in the Puranas abstained from sex. But the rest were fully engaged in polygamy, polyandry and highly liberal sexual unions. For ancient Hindus, sex was not a shameful or forbidden act.

But all this changed after the arrival of Islamic Invaders who forbid polyandry and Christian colonisers who believed in sex as the original sin. Hindu temples containing erotic sculptures became a great embarrassment for Hindus after the sixteenth century. Sexual education became a big taboo. Studying the Hindu Puranas, where the sexual desires of gods are narrated, became a great embarrassment. Modern-day Hindus shy away from their religion because Hindu scriptures contain sexual acts which were sacred for the earlier Hindus but an embarrassment for modern-day Hindus. All this is due to the mindset change that happened in Hindus because of the influence of the original sin believers who ruled as colonists.

There was a famous artist, a painter called M.F. Husain. He was a Muslim who lived in India, who drew pictures of Hindu goddesses the way they were praised in the Sanskrit language. But a number of Hindus felt ashamed because Husain drew a picture of the Hindu goddess Saraswati with a naked chest. This caused cognitive dissonance in the minds of confused Hindus influenced by the thought of original sin. They felt ashamed not because the artist Hussain drew the goddess as she was praised in Sanskrit but because they could not see their goddess, as they carried the shame introduced by original sin. And they forced Husain out of the country. Tragically, Husain migrated to another country and died there.

But my point is to demonstrate that any weaponisation will profoundly impact society, and for centuries has continued to yield power to exploitative individuals. Exploitative humans do not just cause misery to poor people; they affect the lives of rich people like Husain and force them to cross borders. Immigration should be seen from this lens as well.

Sex has been weaponised to such an extent that many get shamed for seeking sex outside marriage, for being gay, for being bisexual, for practising polygamy, for practising polyandry or for being liberal while satiating their sexual need. Many famous people such as ex American President Bill Clinton, Hunter Biden, the son of the current US President Joe Biden, Hindu Swamy Nityananda, UK Labour politician Keith Vaz and many more famous people were all brought down. Their lives were destabilised by shaming them for their sexual adventurism.

Sexual misconduct is different from sexual liberalism. I am only pointing out the weaponisation aspect of sex. Sexual liberalism does not mean we must permit sexual misconduct. My point is that as long as two adults are involved in consensual sex, inside or outside marriage, no one should use the individual's sexual act as a weapon to shame. Yet, I see a pattern in today's human society that takes great pleasure in printing sexual scandals on front pages, reading, and debating about it for weeks on mainstream television shows!

Who told humans that having sex is wrong? That having multiple sexual partners is wrong?! The answer, I believe, is exploitative humans who started using sex as a weapon.

Thus, sex, a natural human need, has been thoroughly controlled, weaponised, shamed, forbidden and used by exploitive humans. This collective sexual assault on humanity has to end. Humans should be allowed to remain humans.

WEAPONISATION OF MARRIAGE

The mediaeval states weaponised the purpose of marriage to confiscate properties. The law, which says that if you are married and your spouse dies, you will be entitled to inherit their property, was entirely created to confiscate the individual's properties. Modern governments distribute the tax they collect as benefits to their citizens. Modern states regulate marriage for no other reason than for taxation purposes.

For instance, during the early twentieth century in South Africa, the ruling government felt people were claiming too many wives, and to collect taxation, they brought in legislation making all marriages illegal, resulting in a citizens' revolt. This is known as the Black Marriages Act of 1909. This law defined marriage as a union between a man and a woman who were both white. This meant that marriages between Indians, who were considered to be non-white, were not legally recognised.

Mahatma Gandhi opposed the Black Marriages Act, arguing that it was discriminatory and violated the rights of Indian people in South Africa..[26] This law effectively rendered all Indian marriages in South Africa invalid, and Gandhi argued that it was a violation of the rights of Indian citizens. He also believed that the law was discriminatory and unfair and led a civil disobedience campaign against it. The law defined marriage as "a union between one man and one woman, entered into in accordance with the rites and ceremonies of the Christian religion." This definition effectively excluded all Indian marriages. Both Hindus and Muslims, till that time, practised polygamy. Some tribes of Hindus and Africans practice polyandry, where a woman can have multiple spouses.

The Black Marriages Act of 1909 aimed to collect more revenues. A part of the administration was dedicated to finding various ways of increasing government revenues. Modern democracies have no such purpose. They announce annual budgets, and everyone knows who is taxed for what. But punitive weaponised instruments are still in existence, causing untold misery to many.

Power should never fall into the wrong hands. But who would be the judge of it? Who dictates right and wrong? Going by ancient human wisdom, any act that causes even a small bit of harm or misery to an individual or a group of individuals is wrong!

In the early twentieth century, the South African government said having multiple wives was not allowed. This caused immediate misery to the Muslim community and Hindu communities in South Africa. Both Muslims and Hindus protested. Muslims stood their ground, whereas Hindus gave up their religious right to marry multiple times. Hindus in India gave up this right in 1955. Hindus had practised polygamy since the beginning. Though Hindu scriptures support this practice, Hindu gods have many wives. Hindus were forced to go against their religion through the Hindu marriage act of 1955. The marriage act says that a marriage is void if it is solemnised between a person who is already married to another person[27]. There is nothing Hindu in this Hindu marriage act. Today many Hindus face severe harassment for having multiple wives even though their religion permits it and allows an individual is free to choose the happiness they deserve in married life. This is what I consider the weaponisation of marriage.

The state has no business regulating marriage! The original intent of the governments behind the Marriage Act was to collect more revenue. Therefore, they weaponised the institution of marriage by bringing it under government regulation.

Causing misery and looting the property of individuals sitting outside the government was the sole intent of most of the colonial governments during past centuries. Every colonised nation was stripped bare of its prosperity. The maharajas of British India were cash cows and toothless tigers for their colonial masters. The British Raj weaponised the marriage law to confiscate the Maharajas' properties.

If the intention of the government behind the marriage governance was to do what was right, then they failed. People like you and me govern the government. That means a group of individuals sitting inside the government is causing misery to the individuals sitting outside the government. But is that the intent of modern democratic governments?! Certainly not.

To achieve their objectives of looting the wealth, colonisers used weaponised instruments like the institution of marriage against the people they were governing. Unfortunately, these weaponised instruments were left intact when colonists left, but weapons of government remained in place. Many African nations and former colonies around the world inherited these weaponised governance structures. They struggled to understand why they didn't work. For example, looking at independent India. It has inherited the weaponised government structures prone to corruption, because of which most of its administration remained corrupt till today! This is why many Indians remain in poverty even today.

FOOD IS WEAPONISED

People have different food habits. Some are vegetarian, and others like to eat meat. But governments controlling what a citizen can or cannot eat has given rise to exploitation. For example, in some countries eating pork is forbidden. Eating beef, especially cow meat, is forbidden in some other countries. But just as how our thumbprints are so unique, our food habits also vary. So why impose our likes and dislikes on food over others?!

I acknowledge religious texts asked for these prohibitions. But my question is, why should governments enforce these?! Is religion not a personal choice of each individual?

Seeds are genetically modified, so any farmer who cultivates using those seeds pays money to the commercial company that patented those seeds. And if the farmer does not pay, the companies genetically modifying the food can drag the farmer to court.

All this is exploitation. No comprehensive studies have been undertaken to understand the impact of these genetic modifications on other species and the environment.

COLONISATION OF FOOD

Before colonisation, Africans ate millet, meat and local produce. Their locally sourced food was nourishing. But colonialists introduced wheat. and sold it. This slowly changed the food habits of the local African population.

But wheat is a crop that does not grow locally. Like all food plants, wheat requires certain geographical conditions to grow. Wheat grows abundantly in the north. Therefore, many African countries spend a significant amount of their GDP on importing wheat.

PET FOOD

We humans have had dogs and cats as pets since the days when we were hunter-gatherers. We used to give our them leftovers, and our pets used to eat what we ate.

But since the expansion of the billions of dollars worth of the pet food industry, we have been discouraged from giving pets our food. In some countries, people can go to jail for feeding pets what they eat!

There must be a statistical review of all laws regulating food worldwide. What food are we advocating, and what food are we discouraging? Why, for what reasons? Is there a commercial industry that has directly benefited due to the change in the law? What was the lobbyist doing? Why were the lawmakers lobbied to change the law? Who is the ultimate beneficiary? If commercial establishments are benefitting from the change of law, then we must question the benefits citizens receive.

DISAPPEARANCE OF NATURALLY SCENTED FLOWERS

Until the mid-nineteenth century, there used to be abundant naturally fragranced flowers in many parts of the world in many gardens and countryside. But there is a worldwide rise of billions of dollars in the commercial scents and fragrance industry. I see a remarkable correlation between the disappearance of naturally scented flowers from public parks or private gardens and the rise of the commercial fragrance industry. We now see flowers with no fragrance everywhere!

HEALTHCARE IS WEAPONISED

Humans are organic matter. They are prone to diseases. Every human deserves to be healthy. But many medicines are prohibitively expensive. Patents on medicines have become instruments of exploitation.

Many poor countries cannot afford to buy essential medicines. Why? Because patents prohibit them from manufacturing those medicines locally. Also, exploitative individuals benefit themselves by not allowing medicines to be sold at reasonable prices.

For example, in the USA, there is a drug called Darapri. It used to be available for US$13.50 in the market. But a start-up company called Turing Pharmaceuticals, run by a former hedge fund manager, bought the company and immediately raised the price to a whopping $750, making the annual cost of treatment for some patients hundreds of thousands of dollars[28]. In another instance, Rodelis Therapeutics acquired a company that makes a drug called Cycloserine, a drug used to treat dangerous multidrug-resistant tuberculosis. But they increased the price from $500 to $10,800 after its acquisition. It was rolled back later from this insane 2,000% price jump[29]. There are many instances worldwide where pharma companies have increased the price of a drug, causing misery to many families who cannot afford it.

However many innocent reasons Pharmaceutical company bosses give for the insane rise of prices, the bottom line is that many humans can not afford healthcare. Pharmaceutical companies, just like any other companies, which are traded in stock markets or privately owned, are controlled by their shareholders. Shareholders seek profits and dividends. They keep putting pressure on the CxOs of the companies to generate profits. Unfortunately, these shareholders do not realise the consequences of their actions on humanity.

Also, in developing countries, another type of exploitation troubles their citizens. Doctors intentionally diagnose their patients with the wrong diseases, to make their patients spend an insane amount of money on cures for diseases which were never there.

In developing countries, maintaining healthcare records is a difficult task. In computer databases, information governance is difficult for managers. Data integrity is extremely important for information governors. Data integrity suffers from two types of prominent problems, namely a commission problem and an omission problem.

In 'commission', record generators intentionally edit a record and insert information which was not there. For example, editing a patient's health record and inserting false information that the patient is suffering from a life-threatening disease is called a 'data integrity breach by the commission'. They allegedly do this to make money from the patient. In India, many news stories came to light where families allege that hospitals kept charging for treatment even after the death of the patient.

In 'omission' they remove a part of the information from the record. If a patient died, they must have recorded this death information. But removing that information automatically kicks in the treatment. Doctors keep treating the patient because the record of death is not there! In India a family accused that the hospital charged them a lot of money for the treatment though their relative died on arrival into the hospital.

The lack of explicit provisions to protect the poor is a great issue in healthcare. People who cannot pay their hospital bills get routinely detained in many countries.

Profiting from the ill health of others is exploitation. But exploiters do not see it that way. Regulation does not help because the country and borders limit regulatory bodies. We need borderless medicines and affordable healthcare for all humans.

Healthcare is of two types: preventative and curative. Following basic hygiene such as brushing teeth regularly, drinking clean water, breathing fresh air, doing daily exercise, and consuming healthy food are all preventive healthcare. They help a person to stay healthy. But this should not be the responsibility of any government! Preventative healthcare is the responsibility of every individual. But the persons who do not look after their health and those who do not take reasonable care to stay healthy fall into exploitative and stupid areas of the four quadrants of human action.

Imagine a person who continues to smoke despite knowing smoking is not suitable for health. What must that person be thinking?! He is helping himself because he finds happiness in smoking. But what happens after his health fails? That person expects others to fund his healthcare so that he can get cured, thus taking away others' money to cure. Is that not ruining others? That person is helping himself and ruining others. Therefore, that person is an exploitative individual.

Healthcare is not required for those who are healthy or those who are dead. Healthcare is required by only those who are sick. Please do a 'spending vs profits' statistical analysis on worldwide healthcare. You will see that an increasing number of people have been get sick over the last three decades. And profits of the healthcare businesses are soaring! This is not healthy for humanity.

Some governments collect taxes, borrow money, or sell the country's natural resources and raise money for public welfare. But the individuals who are in government and private individuals in power become rich but do not provide those amenities for which they borrowed money. These are exploitative structures.

My question to the world's free thinkers is: why and for what reason do modern-day democratic states continue to hold all these weaponised human needs? To exert control? If so, for what purpose?!

As per the multidimensional poverty index (MPI), 16.4% of people in India are poor. But it is not the fault of those people. It is the fault of the remainder of the population, who, due to their sheer ignorance, allow weaponised colonial governance structures to govern. Corruption and weaponised governance structures keep ruining many African countries and countries in Latin America. But the ruling elite in these countries did not just get corrupt overnight! They inherited an exploitative governance structure. Those who drink alcohol get intoxicated, and those who rule people using colonial exploitative governance structures get corrupt.

The objective of modern democratic governments is different. We have a new generation of politically enlightened individuals coming to democratic power through elections. But they are failing and unable to offer their people peace, love and prosperity.

Most governments' actions cause misery to a section of the population, so they are fleeing their countries. In developed countries, governments also cause misery to a section of their people, but these victims silently suffer.

A comprehensive review of all instruments of governments across the world is required. What was the purpose behind initially introducing any law? Is it causing misery? If so, does that instrument needs to exist? If the purpose is still valid, can it be achieved using other modern-day methods or not? There is no answer to greed, but we can certainly address the needs of people worldwide! Democracy is of the people, for the people and by the people. We require a worldwide single borderless democracy for our future evolution as humans.

VALUE DETERMINATION AND WEAPONISATION

Humans began their journey of exchanging goods in a barter system. In the barter system, each participant used to determine the value they attached to their goods. For example, one person may barter one bread loaf for one blanket, whereas another person may barter two bread loaves. Thus the value changes from person to person.

Even today, the value attachment has not changed. But we have centralised fiat currencies, which help control and regulate the market so that exploitative forces will not take advantage of market conditions to make unreasonable gains. For example, a scarcity of wheat in a region automatically forces up the price of wheat to make more profit. Regulatory controls help control such actions. But because the world is divided into various countries with borders, regulations fail across the borders.

Also, fiat currencies are manipulated by banks. All banks combined together know in each country how much money is in circulation. But they only share this data with their country. Some countries keep this data secret.

As a result, inequality prevails, contributing to human misery. For example, due to the war in Ukraine, wheat-dependent African nations spent more than 60% of their income on buying wheat.

MODERN-DAY WEALTH FLOW

The US media company Netflix has a large user subscription base in the UK. But it is criticised for paying only a limited amount of tax in the UK. Netflix paid just £5.2 million in 2021 and £4 million in 2020 as tax, though it earned a reported revenue of £1.3 billion in 2021 and £1.5 billion in 2020. At the same time, the same Netflix company reportedly paid an estimated US $100 million to ex-Prince Harry and his wife Megan for their story. So the wealth, instead of getting paid as tax, went straight into the pockets of two individuals with an exciting story to tell. Netflix has not disclosed the exact amount of money it paid for their multi-year deal. The question is, who decides that the value of this story is going to be this much?

PLANNED OBSOLESCENCE

Similarly, some businesses pay huge bonuses and dividends, creating wealth distribution inequality. In order to satisfy the greed of the shareholders, business owners adopt controversial strategies. One of these strategies is called Planned Obsolescence. Modern-day rapid industrial production systems are capable of producing products in huge numbers. But consumers have to be available to consume these products.

In the mid twentieth century, a brilliant young engineer opened a shaving blades factory. After a few years of production, the sales had slumped. The owner had conducted market research, thinking that consumers might have lost interest in his product, which is why the sales had slumped. But to his surprise, all consumers of his shaving blades gave glorifying reviews. It perplexed the business owner. If consumers loved his product, why were they not buying it? Why was the popularity of his product not turning into profitability? After doing multiple market research studies, he finally found that his product was so brilliantly designed and engineered that it did not deteriorate. The steel material used in his product was of brilliant quality, meaning that each shaving blade his factory created would last for thousands of shaves. Therefore it was recommended to him that to increase the sales of his shaving blades, he should design blades that would only last a few shaves. This is called planned obsolescence, a strategy where products are designed to become obsolete or unusable after a certain period of time so that consumers have to buy new ones. Today's shaving blades are designed to last only a few shaves, and we have to buy new ones…

Many modern-day consumer products, such as light bulbs, cars, cell phones, etc., are designed and marketed with planned obsolescence in mind. Planned obsolescence gives profits and dividends to the company's shareholders but causes enormous environmental damage due to waste and landfills. Modern-day businesses are overtly serving the interests of some forces. But serving the interests of limited individuals must be a second priority to serving the taxpayers.

TAXATION WEAPONISED

Global tax havens are weaponised exploitative instruments. But at the same time, the taxation structures do not make sense in many countries.

A simple rule is that if one lives and does business in a country, then one must pay taxes. But many companies do business in the country, but to save taxes, they pay taxes in another country. This is exploitation. It may not be a crime in the eyes of the law, but for sure, it causes destabilisation of humanity.

Due to their exploitative colonial structures, many governments offer business contracts for unnecessary reasons. This means citizens get taxed for services they do not need.

There must be a global awakening on all government spending because spending leads to borrowing at higher interest rates or taxes.

8

FREEDOM FOR EVERYONE

"A wife loves her husband not for his sake, but for her own sake. A husband loves his wife not for her sake, but for his own sake. Parents love their children not for the sake of the children, but for their own sake. People love wealth not for its sake, but for their own sake. Thinkers and teachers are loved, not for their sake, but for the sake of the Self. Warriors and kings are loved, not for their sake, but for the sake of the Self. The Gods, the worlds, the beings in the world, and everything else - they are not loved for their sake, but for the sake of the Self. Indeed, you must realise the Self. Hear it, reflect upon it, and meditate upon it."

Brihadaranyaka Upanishad (2.4.1-5)

HUMAN-DRAWN BORDERS HURTING HUMANITY

All countries must come together to create a truly borderless earth. Exploitation will continue as long as countries keep their structures.

For example, imagine a country called Country A which has high-tech weapons. It is highly advanced. And using its firepower, brain power, and all sorts of power structures at its disposal, it enforces protectionist measures. The country's trade policies with the rest of the world are driven by the value it can gain for its citizens. This limitation in objectives may help Country A, but is bound to create imbalance and injustice in some other countries.

Imagine Country B is negatively affected by the activities of Country A. All citizens of County B will apply to migrate to Country A. What happens then?!

Please use the Four Quadrants of Human Activity diagram to plot the international policies of each country. Nearly all of them fall in the exploitative quadrant.

Helping myself (my country) by ruining others (other countries) is the mode of activity for all countries. They do not think that we have only one earth to live upon. They are worried about climate impact, but they address the issue only at a superficial level. They do not address the real elephant in the global living room. All exploitative forces are creating imbalances. Some countries are so corrupt and powerless that they can not enforce anything! I do not see any point in lecturing the world until we do address the exploitative and stupid forces worldwide which are causing these imbalances.

BUTTERFLY EFFECT

The term 'butterfly effect' comes from the exaggerated idea that flapping a butterfly's wings in one part of the world could set off a chain of events that would eventually lead to a tornado in another part of the world. The mathematician and meteorologist Edward Norton Lorenz observed that a slight change in one state of a deterministic nonlinear system could result in significant differences in a later state.

Some exploitative countries' activities, such as fossil fuel projects, put the health and safety of local communities at risk. They often bring dire threats to indigenous people, and to poor and working-class communities. Moreover, they create the butterfly effect, which causes climate chaos in far-off lands. We do not yet have an accurate predictive model available to calculate the butterfly effect that some projects cause.

NO RESOURCE SHOULD BE OWNED BY ANY SINGLE COUNTRY

Our squabbling between countries is causing global distress. We humans are a collective species. We must globally own the resources while respecting the rights and aspirations of the people who are looking after these resources. We must have a global trustee model for each and every resource. The governance should span the laws of all countries.

NOT A CALL FOR REVOLUTION

Humans without Borders is not a call for revolution but a humble petition to evolve. It is a suggestion for a natural evolution. Fortunately, this evolution is already in progress. The rigid exploitative governance structures, which served their purpose, started collapsing after the 1950s. Humans in some developed countries started feeling freedom.

If we acknowledge that all humans have equal freedom, then one person's freedom should not become another person's misery. As I wrote earlier in the book, each person is unique. Our thumbprints are unique. Our psychological makeup is unique. Therefore it is tantamount to stupidity to expect another person to fall in line. It won't happen. People submit themselves out of fear of exploitative individuals. But one person who does not fear waves the flag of revolt, eventually bringing down the mightiest of dictators. This is how revolutions happened, and they continue to happen.

Freedom does not mean imposing our will on others or forcing others to accept our behaviour. Freedom means peace naturally arising from non-violent behaviour at all levels of human personality. In absolute freedom, there won't be an argument about racism because any person who is established in freedom will instantly recognise that it is stupid to harbour racist thoughts. In absolute freedom, there won't be exploitation.

There have been people in the past who have shown us what real freedom means. You may see Moses, Jesus Christ, Prophet Muhammad, Zarathustra, Buddha, Mahavir, Adi Shankara, Ramanuja, Madhava and other enlightened individuals as religious leaders and prophets. But I think they are real freedom fighters, fearless humans with extraordinary character. Similarly, Aristotle, Plato, Galileo and countless other philosophers and scientific visionaries are freedom fighters.

For example, look at Moses' Ten Commandments. Out of them, five commandments are commonly professed by other religions too. Indeed, the prophets I mentioned above had them embedded in their teachings. Honour your father and your mother; you shall not murder, You shall not steal, You shall not bear false witness against your neighbour, and You shall not covet, all these commandments are to be found as teachings. These commandments are easy to grasp and plain to understand. If all humans voluntarily follow these five commandments, they will put us in the right-side quadrants of the four modes of the human activity diagram. It makes all followers of the commandments as ordinary humans and altruistic humans.

Thou shall not commit murder: How easy it is to follow, but worldwide, every day, we read stories of bloodbaths, and people do murder.

At the beginning of this chapter, I quoted a verse from the Hindu Upanishad about love. A seer called Rishi Yaajnavalkya speaks it. He asked the individual to reflect on why the individual is so self-centred.

When the food we eat is common, the air we breathe is common, and the water we drink is common, where is the sense of self coming from? Any individual who reflects on this more profound truth becomes an evolved soul. Altruism stems from such exalted states of evolved minds. We must encourage all children to think as a global collective.

UNIVERSAL FAMILY

We become a universal family if we achieve absolute freedom for all humanity, as humans without borders. We humans are already universal in our individual thinking. We are advancing in space exploration. But on earth, though we are universally connected, we are acting as order-based countries instead of as a family. As countries, we conspire against each other, slaughtering each other in wars. But if we bring forth the concept of love and compassion, then we end the reason for war. In ancient days, rival clans got married to each other to make them a single family to cease hostilities and achieve permanent peace. We must apply the principle of love to stop all exploitations.

Since it is human nature to be exploitative sometimes and to be altruistic at other times, we can not stop people when they act in the left side of the quadrant to dominate, and cause harm to the humans on the right side of the quadrant The option that comes to my mind is to help each other evolve. All countries must have policies which help evolve humanity into a universal family full of peace, love, and prosperity. Policies must aim to remove the instruments available to exploit, and to stop stupid action in its tracks.

But how to achieve these things?

To start with, we must cease to be countries with borders. There have been a number of projects that are already helping humanity progress towards a Universal Family. Projects such as the European Union, the African Union, The League of Arab States (LAS), The Association of Southeast Asian Nations (ASEAN), The Shanghai Cooperation Organization (SCO) and others are aimed towards becoming a family.

EUROPEAN UNION

The EU has a single market. It allows the free movement of goods, capital, services, and people between member states. The EU also has a common currency, the euro, which is used by 19 member states. The EU has several common policies, including a common agricultural policy, a common fisheries policy, and a common foreign and security policy. The EU is a major economic and political power in the world. The EU's economy is the largest in the world, and the EU is a major player in international trade. The EU is also a major player in international diplomacy and security.

AFRICAN UNION

The African Union (AU) is a continental union consisting of 55 member states located on the continent of Africa. The AU has helped resolve several conflicts on the continent, including the conflict in Darfur. It has also helped to promote economic growth and development, and to promote democracy and human rights.

PROBLEMS FACED BY THESE UNIONS

There are many such unions between various countries. But such unions have been criticised for their bureaucracy, lack of transparency, and undemocratic decision-making process. Each union faces a number of specific challenges. For example, the African

Union faces a number of challenges, including poverty, hunger, disease, and conflict where, whereas the European Union faces the challenges of terrorism and refugee crisis.

Brexit

I believe countries coming together as unions is a good step towards evolution. Eventually, I wish for all these unions to merge and become a single universal borderless family – as humans without borders.

Many countries within these unions do face problems. But Brexit is an interesting phenomenon. I believe the UK took an exploitative colonial route when it separated from the EU. The professors for Brexit argued that the UK had lost its sovereignty to the EU; they were concerned that the free movement of citizens is causing immigration problems which are affecting the economy. I understand these reasons, but Brexit will not help solve the problems. In fact, the UK has been facing a significant refugee crisis since Brexit. Also, Brexit goes contrary to the vision that the UK publicly proclaims, that they are committed to global peace. How can humans achieve peace as long as we prefer to exist as splintered groups? Half the population of the UK did not want Brexit.

The UK was once a great empire. It ruled nearly 80% of the world. It was called 'the British Empire where the Sun does not set'. Similarly, France and other European countries were colonial powers. These countries were exploitative. They caused enormous economic inequality and pain to the rest of the world. But I believe all these countries, such as the UK and France, have a pearl of acquired wisdom: they knew and documented all these countries and cultures. They are best placed to make the world without borders.

They are best placed to set all humans free. Brexit is a disappointing step back.

Though technologically advanced, the USA lost its compassion over the last seventy years. The nature of American business instead forces people into the exploitative quadrant. The vision of the great founding fathers of the USA does not appear anymore in the actions of any recent leaders of America.

I love the intention behind the great lines whenever I read the American Declaration of Independence. "Prudence, indeed, will dictate that Governments long established should not be changed for light and transient causes; and accordingly all experience hath shewn, that mankind are more disposed to suffer, while evils are sufferable, than to right themselves by abolishing the forms to which they are accustomed…"

I love America for its beautiful landscape, fiercely independent-minded free-spirited citizenry, patriotism, and allowance to provide opportunities for human aspiration. But that great nation has a very dark side to it. Exploitative humans govern this dark side. They caused immense bloodshed during the last half a century.

What we need from America is to help implement the vision of America's Founding Fathers to the whole world. They must stop wars and give love a chance to heal.

All countries must collectively achieve the do the following:

1 Stop the reactive way of governance.

2 Bring absolute transparency in all controlling structures in the public and private sectors.

3 No more secrets.

4 Make the world individual and human-centric. This means each human will become their government. They will be highly independent in his personal life. But all their interactions with any human will be on a public ledger.

This is the actual use case for the already proven technology to achieve this, called Blockchain.

All humans, without exception, must be part of this public ledger to self-balance.

Each human will become free and independent, yet a non-separable part of universal humanity. No more exploitative governance structures. No more scope for individual human stupidity to hurt wider humanity. A proper self-balancing system which offers all humans to only love fellow humans. Show compassion to fellow humans. This system does not allow natural human traits such as greed, jealousy, hate and avarice to act up.

A human can think whatever they want, but when that thought becomes an action, that action falls into one of the four quadrants, which affects fellow humans. The system we propose minimises harmful impact and allows justice.

We must say no to the misuse of advanced technologies. And make sure these technologies are not in the hands of exploitative individuals.

With their power over advanced technologies, exploitative individuals are causing worldwide destabilisation for humanity. None of the technologies that have a pan-global impact on humanity should remain the property or secret of any single country! Anything in space should not be owned by a single country because the secret itself is an exploitative instrument. But we must not encourage stupid activities undertaken by people such as Edward Snowden or others. Edward Snowden was a computer consultant who worked for American National Security Agency (NSA). At that time NSA had computer programs which were aimed at compromising individual security and liberty. Snowden did not like it, so he leaked highly classified information from the National Security Agency in 2013. What NSA doing was wrong, but what Snowden did was also wrong. By his stupid activity, Snowden jeopardised the safety and security of many innocent personal working in various departments of the USA. Violent action never yields long lasting good results for anybody. Two wrongs never make anything right! I understand both NSA and Snowden's positions, but I do not encourage Snowden's kind of activities. We shall have non-violence in our hearts and endeavours. If we want to build a world full of love, peace and prosperity, we must be able to possess it ourselves first.

If we consider there is an intelligent design behind this universe, then we acknowledge it took millions of years of evolution to reach the point where we are. So why hurry?!

We are in such a mad rush to bring order to our surroundings that we get easily upset and angry if things don't go the way we planned. We must check our cognitive dissonance. We get disappointed because we make futile appointments with the future. Snowden was in such a rush to bring about change that he compromised the security of many!

We must stop rushing society. There are altruistic human leaders across the world. We must bring them together as a forum. Plead with them. Slowly there will be change. We may see this change happening in a few years, or we may not see this happening for the next generation. But we keep making our point. Slowly and steadily, we will make progress. We can make leaders recognise the exploitation that is taking place and the results that we are witnessing.

A GLOBAL SELF-GOVERNANCE ARCHITECTURE

We can architect a new world that is more suitable to our natural human evolution.

Let us architect a new system that suits our humanity. Let us put the whole earth on a tripod and let it continue its natural spin beautifully! Let us visualise the globe on a tripod which has legs called Peace, Love and Prosperity for each individual inhabitant of this universe.

Peace, Love and Prosperity are concepts subject to various definitions. Still, all humans have a gut feeling about what peace means to us, what love means to us and what prosperity means to us.

So let each individual expand their horizons and wonder. I already know what I mean by peace for me and love and prosperity for myself, but what about the individuals in my immediate circle?! Do they share the same exact definition of peace, love and prosperity?

If not, then the individual is in conflict. This conflict then results in wars. History has proven this again and again. So the Global Governance Architecture, which enables Humans without Borders, will use the new advanced technologies to help humanity in its evolution.

VALUE IN THE NEW ARCHITECTURE

Till today, the world has been governed by a top-down approach, that is, a pyramid structure where rules are enforced by the people at the top over the people at the bottom. Even in democracies, the approach is that there is a leader who represents their people. But as our thumbprints do not match, our thoughts do not match. Each human is unique, travelling alone to the alone all alone. Therefore, each human must be free to act as a master of the universe.

In the new architecture, humanity 2.0, each individual is the master of his universe. If they are a wheat producer, then the value they attach to their produce is always known to the world. Each person, acting as a node, attaches value and also modifies the value.

So this must work on certain principles such as Human-centric, No borders, No countries and No interventions −. but subjected to regulations and controls. Otherwise, human greed and madness are capable of doing the most significant harm.

Our primary objective is to free humanity from the clutches of debilitating exploitative forces. We can achieve this using modern technologies. Our aspiration for a new world is not revolution. We would not destroy anything that exists today. We would not cause violence in achieving our new objectives - Love, Peace and Prosperity for the maximum.

So how do we adapt the existing regulations?

Earlier, I had put the question: if humans were given a choice to roam free and settle in whichever country they wanted, which countries would they choose and why?

It is the attachment of value that drives human aspiration. Each person wants to survive, wants to be happy and wants to know. They aspire to get these in another country because these are not available in their country.

The derivative value is in the human mind. We must now democratise it as if the world was a small village, and all inhabitants must individually know the bartering value each villager attaches to the specific goods and services on offer.

The problem which humanity is facing today is the structure of countries. Large land masses are sitting on resources equally required by all humans. But the policies which these countries enact causing large-scale destabilisation in aspirational human mindset.

Humanity can survive if all exploitative forces stop influencing the world's financial systems.

Therefore, in the new world, taxation should be calculated person by person. There is no need for top-down flat 30% or 40% tax structures. Data is available for each individual. There has to be a will to share happiness with the rest of the world.

SIDE-BUS ARCHITECTURE TO TEST

Any endeavour we make towards guiding our evolution must be non-violent. It must be safe and comfortable to adapt.

Imagine each country that we live in as a bus. Basically, we are all travelling in 195 different buses, which are all engaged in a mad race to be ahead, God knows to reach where. The first seven, who are way ahead in this race, are called the G7, and when we include the next thirteen, we call them the G20.

We propose that they must disengage from this mad race. But how? By adapting a 'side bus' architecture. We create a single bus which runs in parallel to all these 195 buses.

ABSOLUTE FREEDOM FOR EACH AND EVERY HUMAN

As a unique self-serving centre, each human has a right only to their boundary. For example, if a person is a vegetarian, they must not expect to impose their views on others in any way but should respect people's feelings. They can remain vegetarian, and others can be non-vegetarian.

The problem with today's society is that governments are struggling hard to create an inclusive society. The idea of creating highly tolerant, inclusive societies is brilliant. However, they are highly unnatural. The imposition of laws which governments adapt to make such a society possible only create more opportunities for exploitative and stupid human actions, leading to more misery. Eventually, all societies collapse because they are artificially created against our true human nature. We are born free. All species are born free. Anything that enslaves us causes us misery. We become unhappy, and we do everything and anything to be happy again.

A human has absolute rights over their life. No one should impose. But free humans should also fully own responsibility for any consequences of their actions. Nobody should be burdened with the irresponsibility of others. For example, humans who deliberately destroy their health should not become the burden of other individuals. Each human must be free to choose what they want to do, and this includes the fact that it must be their responsibility if they wish to submit themselves to a leader.

Today's world has too many laws which stifle human freedom. True freedom is to breathe like a human, think like a human, and not think within the parameters set by exploitative individuals who have set up exploitative structures. The results are visible. There is mad violence, wars, arson and thievery across the world. This suggests that we

brought stupid outcomes by splintering ourselves as divided nations –
that is, that we not only ruined ourselves but also ruined others.

One of the founding fathers of America, George Washington, said
that 'Freedom and Property Rights are inseparable. You can't have
one without the other.' I think that is a pearl of great wisdom. We
humans want to own. But how can we own without causing hurt to
others? There are some modern-day thinkers who believe that
humans must own nothing. They believe that by removing
ownership, we can remove unhappiness. But unhappiness is
psychological. It is not caused by physically having something or not.
Therefore, I think that instead of 'you own nothing and you will be
happy', everyone must own everything, like shareholders of a
business who have a collective interest. Every human must be a
shareholder of the earth.

The architecture of a new human society of this kind would remove
the burden on other humans to accept all imposed laws arbitrarily.
Imagine, for example, that because I am a vegetarian, I get the law
changed so that no one can criticise my vegetarianism and no meat
can be served on a table where I sit. Such a law would make me
happy but make an unknown number of individuals miserable. They
would immigrate to countries where such suffocating laws do not
exist.

The government's intention behind creating such laws is laudable.
But I believe they are contrary to natural evolution. We must aim to
free every human. The laws are archaic. They served their purpose:
to let each human live close to their uniquely true nature. With the
advance of technology, this is possible today. We need the
decentralisation of each human from countries, government
structures, and every imposing structure.

The structures today are designed to contain and control. The new design will reverse this. Each human must become a self-centred containment and control structure. Each human is their own government. Each human is the master governor of his own country. Each human is free and bears the consequences of their exploitative or stupid actions.

This new structure requires a paradigm shift, a new way of thinking. The huge question is, who is going to govern if each human is free? This question comes from the mindset which is so used to the control and containment of other humans.

Technology can attach skills, possessions, and everything that gives each human a unique identity. But we will be the ones who design the new architecture, which gives a new way of looking at these.

THE QUESTION OF EVIL

Are the exploitative individuals evil?! The word 'evil' is the reverse of the word 'live', when you spell it backwards. I wonder where evil is. Its act seems only to extinguish life. But life gets continuously extinguished in front of our eyes every moment in the natural course of things … Matter can not be destroyed. We see matter being recycled. And consciousness is all-pervading, like space. Perhaps we are like fish swimming in the ocean of consciousness? What we see are the limitations in our vision. So is death an act of evil? It can't be. So where is evil?!

Evil, on the other hand, is in how we witness death and other negative occurrences and give psychological energy to them. Evil is not death but the unbearable ruthless, narcissistic, psychopathic, sociopathic, Machiavellian kind of tormenting others while they are alive. Evil is the creation of humans. Human thoughts which wickedly plan to torment others are evil. Humans are capable of evil energy. Death, in contrast, puts an end to it. Therefore, what we humans are responsible for creating we must be able to control, in order to put an end to it if necessary. Humans must put an end to all evil thoughts and actions so that this world becomes a better place for everyone to live in.

FORGIVENESS

Even the worst evildoer can one day become a good person due to a change of heart. We must give that chance to humanity. Forgiveness gives us humans that much breathing space. It allows nature to heal the damage.

A section of humankind has always been involved in exploitation since the beginning. Exploitative actions are inevitable. We cannot banish them because exploitative activities emerge from the primitive prehistoric mindset. As hunter-gatherers, we were constantly exposed to dangers and therefore exploitative nature helped us to survive.

It is time we evolved to the next level of our human evolution. Stop judging people based on their eating habits, sleeping habits, sexual habits and phobias. Laws created to control these four have been weaponised for centuries and have only led to enslavement.

There has to be liberty for all beings.

REFERENCES

1. Jung, C. (n.d.). *Civilisation in Transition*. New York: Pantheon Books, p.154.

2. Internet Archive. (2017). *Bhagavad Gita Bhashyam of Adi Sankara - Sanskrit Text Only (2 PDFs)* pp. 63 [online] Available at: https://archive.org/details/BhagavadGitaBhashyaAdiSankara2/Bhagavad%20Gita%20Bhashya%20Adi%20Sankara%201/page/n155/mode/2up [Accessed 20 Jun. 2023].

3. Tagore, R. (n.d.). [online] New York: Macmillan, pp.70–71. Available at: https://poets.org/poem/gitanjali-35/print.

4. Mādhavānanda, S. (n.d.). The Bṛhadāraṇyaka Upaniṣad (with the Commentary of Śaṅkarācārya). pp. 86-87 [online] Available at: https://archive.org/details/Brihadaranyaka.Upanishad.Shankara.Bhashya.by.Swami.Madhavananda/page/86/mode/2up.

5. Ved, V. (n.d.). THE BRAHMANDA PURANA PART. 1. [online] DELHI: MOTILAL BANARSIDASS PUBLISHERS PVT., pp.9–10. Available at: https://archive.org/details/dli.bengal.10689.21603/page/n21/mode/2up.

6. Assagioli, R. (n.d.). *Psychosynthesis and the act of will*. New York: Viking Press, p.15.

7. mythologian. (n.d.). Sri Yantra/Sri Chakra Symbol (Shree Yantra) and Its Meaning. [online] Available at: https://mythologian.net/mythology/shree-yantra/ [Accessed 21 Jun. 2023].

8.   Internet Archive. (2017). *Bhagavad Gita Bhashyam of Adi Sankara - Sanskrit Text Only (2 PDFs)* pp. 104 [online] Available at: https://archive.org/details/BhagavadGitaBhashyaAdiSankar a2/Bhagavad%20Gita%20Bhashya%20Adi%20Sankara%20 1/page/n103/mode/2up [Accessed 20 Jun. 2023].

9.   Moran, Lord. (1945). The anatomy of courage. London: Constable, pp. 13-14.

10. Lao Tzu. (2009). Tao Te Ching. Translated by Stephen Mitchell. New York: Harper Perennial Modern Classics, p.127.

11. Brown, R. M. (1983). Sudden Death. New York: Bantam Books, p.123.

12. Anonymous. (n.d.). We do not see things as they are. We see them as we are. [Paraphrase of a passage from the Talmud]. Retrieved from https://www.goodreads.com/quotes/5030- we-don-t-see-things-as-they-are-we-see-them There is no specific source for the quote in the Talmud. The quote is more likely a paraphrase of a passage from the Talmud that says: "The eyes of man are windows to his soul, and what he sees reflects what he is." (Bava Metzia 58b)

13. Festinger, L. (1975). A theory of cognitive dissonance. Stanford, CA: Stanford University Press, p.3.

14. Wikipedia Contributors (2019). Jallianwala Bagh massacre. [online] Wikipedia. Available at: https://en.wikipedia.org/wiki/Jallianwala_Bagh_massacre.

15. Hill, E. (2020). How George Floyd was killed in police custody. The New York Times. [online] 31 May. Available at: https://www.nytimes.com/2020/05/31/us/george-floyd- investigation.html.

16. Petrikowski, N. (2019). Charlie Hebdo shooting | Facts, Victims, & Response. In: Encyclopædia Britannica. [online]

Available at: https://www.britannica.com/event/Charlie-Hebdo-shooting.

17. Hammer, A. (2023). Documents reveal two black US soldiers were killed by white colleague. [online] Mail Online. Available at: https://www.dailymail.co.uk/news/article-11638395/Documents-two-black-World-War-Two-soldiers-murdered-white-colleague.html [Accessed 21 Jun. 2023].

18. Speakola. (n.d.). Mahatma Gandhi: 'Non violence is the first article of my faith', Statement in The Great Trial - 1922. [online] Available at: https://speakola.com/political/mahatma-gandhi-the-great-trial-1922.

19. Patnaik, U. (2018). The plunder of India: Britain's role in the destruction of a great civilization. Columbia University Press, p.13.

20. Olusoga, D. (2016). The darkest places on earth: A history of the transatlantic slave trade. Faber & Faber, p.10.

21. Authors: Harcourt, A. H., & Stewart, K. J. (1987). Gorilla reproduction and social behavior. Animal Behaviour, 35(1), 127-147.

22. Author: Lewis, M. E. (1999). The political economy of the early Chinese state. Albany: State University of New York Press, p.137.

23. Augustine. (1950). The city of God. (D. B. Zema & G. G. Walsh, Trans.). The Fathers of the Church: A New Translation, Vol. 8. Washington, DC: Catholic University of America Press. "I have already shown that original sin is transmitted by generation, not by imitation." P.521.

24. Sankaracarya, Suresvaracarya, Madhava, son of C., Mahadeva Sastri, A., Madhava, d 1386 and University of California Libraries (1903). The Taittiriya-upanishad. P.138.

[online] Internet Archive. Mysore : Printed at the C. T. A. Printing Works. Available at: https://archive.org/details/taittiriyaupanis00sankiala/page/136/mode/2up [Accessed 21 Jun. 2023].

25. Wikipedia Contributors (2019). Kama Sutra. [online] Wikipedia. Available at: https://en.wikipedia.org/wiki/Kama_Sutra.

26. Author: Gandhi, M. K. (1909, November 20). The Black Marriages Act. Natal Indian Opinion.

27. Mahawar, S. (2022). Hindu Marriage Act, 1955. [online] iPleaders. Available at: https://blog.ipleaders.in/hindu-marriage-act-1955/#The_marriage_should_be_monogamous [Accessed 21 Jun. 2023].

28. Pollack, A. (2015). Drug Goes From $13.50 a Tablet to $750, Overnight. The New York Times. [online] 20 Sep. Available at: https://www.nytimes.com/2015/09/21/business/a-huge-overnight-increase-in-a-drugs-price-raises-protests.html.

29. NBC News. (n.d.). Price Hike for Tuberculosis Drug Cycloserine Rolled Back From 2,000% Jump. [online] Available at: https://www.nbcnews.com/health/health-news/price-hike-tuberculosis-drug-cycloserine-rolled-back-2-000-jump-n431716.

30. Mādhavānanda, S. (n.d.). The Bṛhadāraṇyaka Upaniṣad (with the Commentary of Śaṅkarācārya). pp. 354-355 [online] Available at: https://archive.org/details/Brihadaranyaka.Upanishad.Shankara.Bhashya.by.Swami.Madhavananda/page/354/mode/2up.